motley mag
death of motley
(issue 4)

First edition: April, 2023

Cover design: João Bresler
Printed somewhere on Earth i hope
ISBN: 978-1-4477-8769-3.

Worm Literature
MMXXIII

Motley Mag

DEATH OF MOTLEY

Editors And Collaborators Of Motley Mag:

EDITOR. João Bresler @oysterboiwho

COLLABORATORS.
(in order of appearance, with the first piece being the guide in case of having contributed with multiple pieces)

	A	B	C
1	Ryan	@wheresmylostdog	5
2	Reagan	@thret_rhett	6
3	Vika	@bon_pardon	8 & 45
4	Crypti	@cryptixotic	9,30,62
5	Mathilde	@longkekmammi	10 & 33
6	Con Essa	@orenjijusuu_	11 & 95
7	Kipper	@peasteef	12
8	Lula	@lullilak	13
9	GACT	@gactome	14
10	Sylvie	@icuffmyjeans	15-18,32,97
11	Brad	@breadpulp	19-23
12	Lucian	@lucian.brb	24,80-82
13	Zee	@myhyperfixation	25 & 26
14	Kumo	@mushroomkumo	27,63,87
15	Helena	@kunstumkunst	28
16	Gabriel	@nachtverhaal	31 & 49
17	Eva	@switchblade.jpeg	34 & 75
18	Terra Zook	@terrazook	35 & 48
19	Lily	@lavindex	36
20	Leo Steele	@cadmium.cabal	37-41
21	Georgie (Warm Wishes)	@warmwishesband	43
22	Donnie	@d0nnster	44
23	Kaia	@liiiblikas	51
24	Hari	@haricore_	52 & 53
25	Sammy	@sikeitssammy	54
26	Guilhèm Berini	@gberinif	56-59
27	Dirt H.	@dirthief	98
28	Elena	@memontecinos	64-66
29	Laysa Schat		67
30	Peio Camara	@peiocamara	68 & 69
31	Zoe Watt	@zoeowatt	72
32	Emlee	@emlee100	74
33	Mark Cheruvallithazhe Philip	@x3n0000	76 & 77
34	Brad Hock	@bardo.bread	78 & 79
35	Jack Bullard	@bowtie.pasta	93
36	Dorottya Faa	@disaaky	99
37	Jorge	chronologyofsounds or geisterbilder on tumblr	107-110
38	Daniel Flores	@choco_mintzzz	111-113
39	João	@oysterboiwho	4,7,42,46,50,55,60,70,71,73, 83-86,88-90,92,94,96,100-10 4

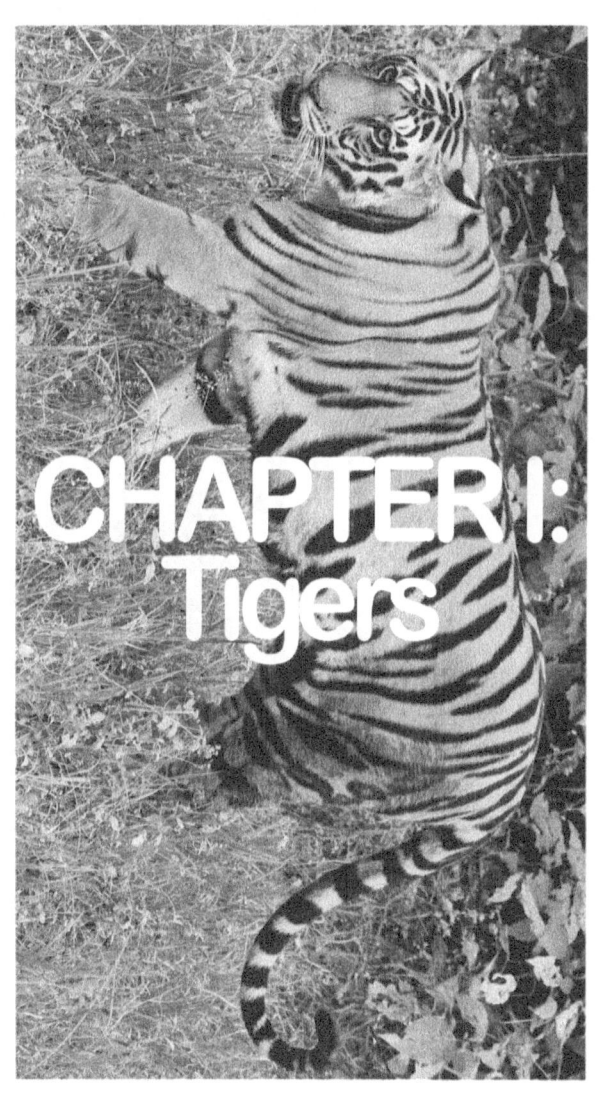

CHAPTER I:
Tigers

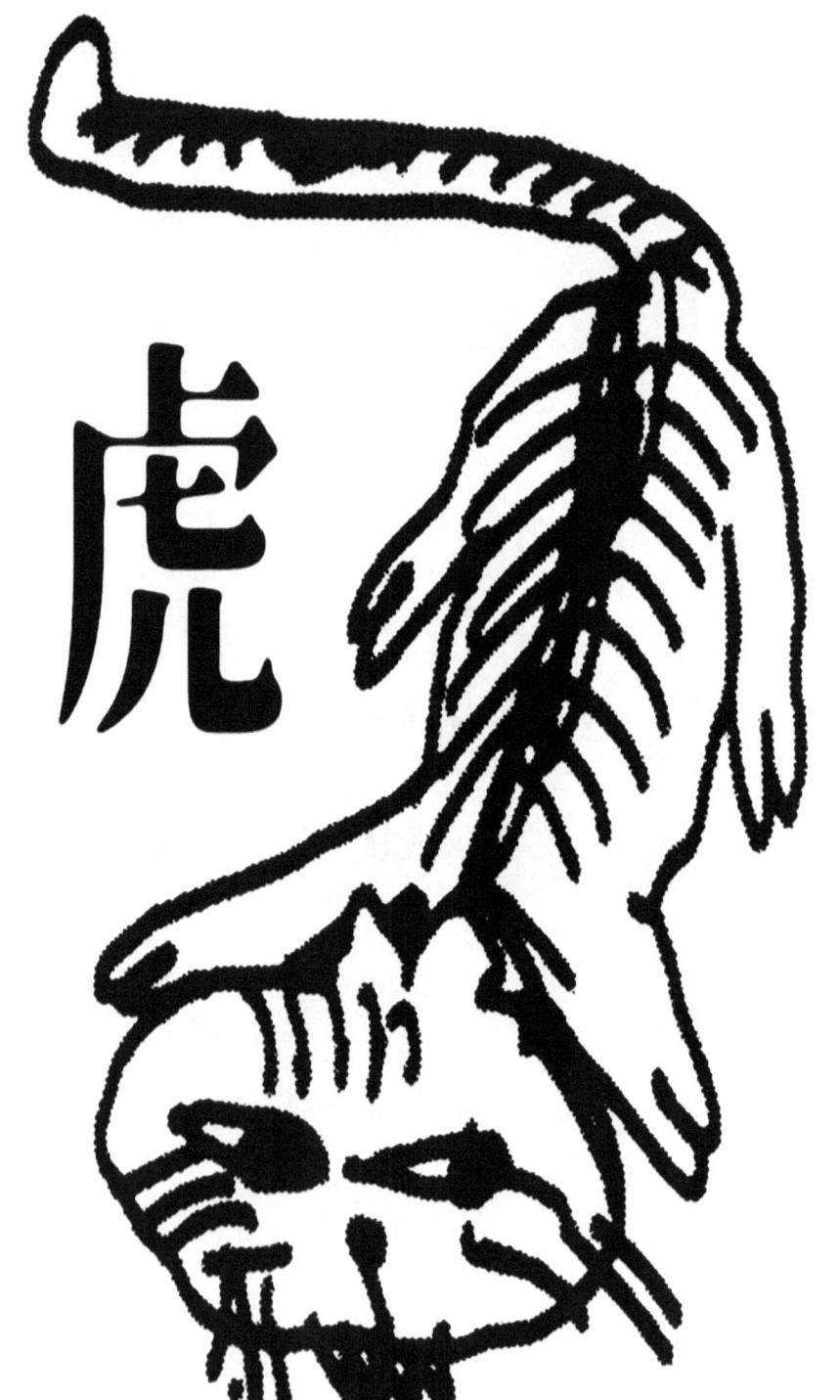

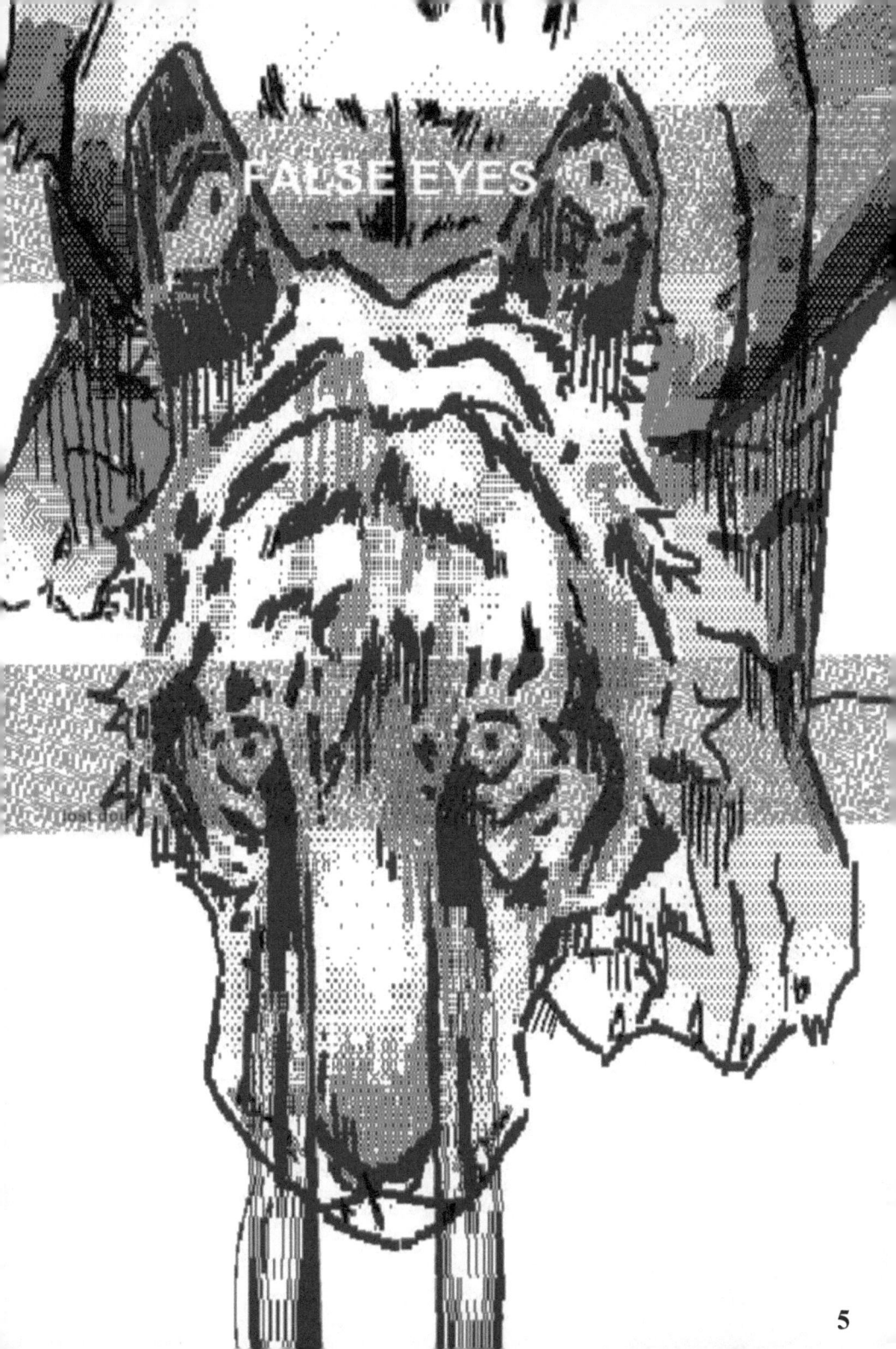

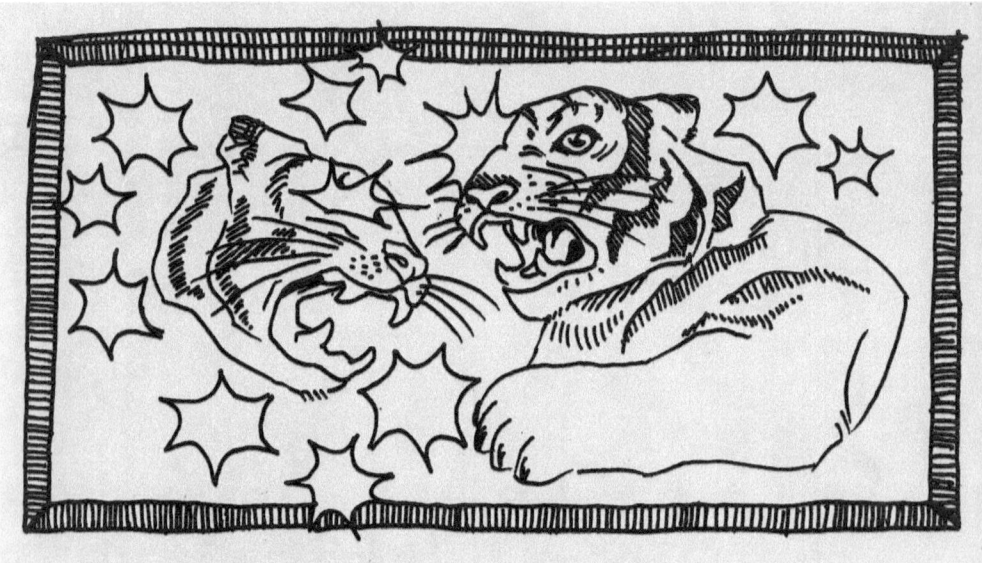

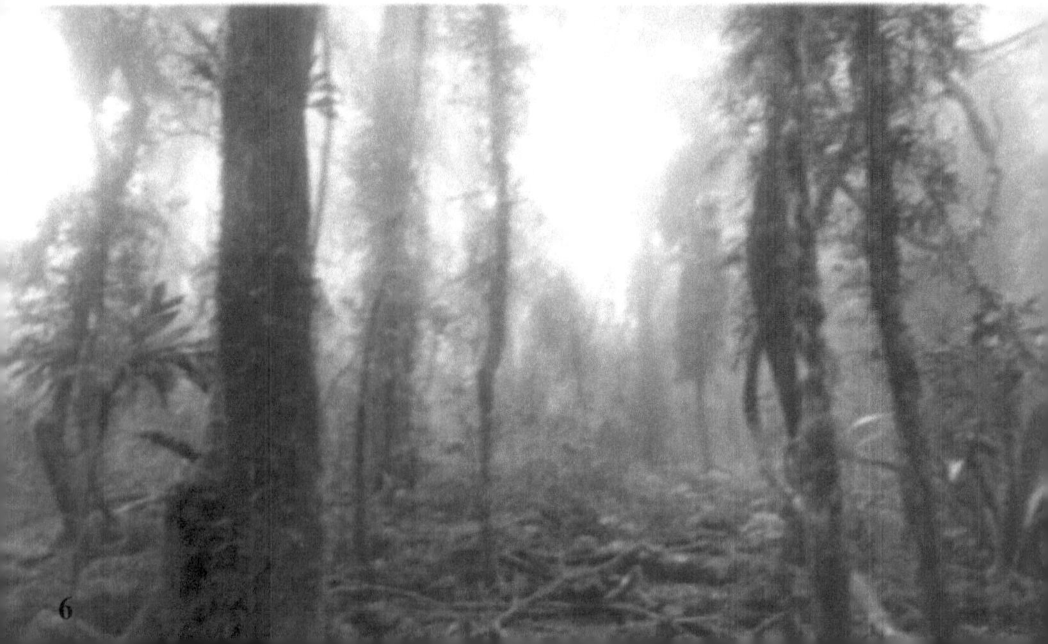

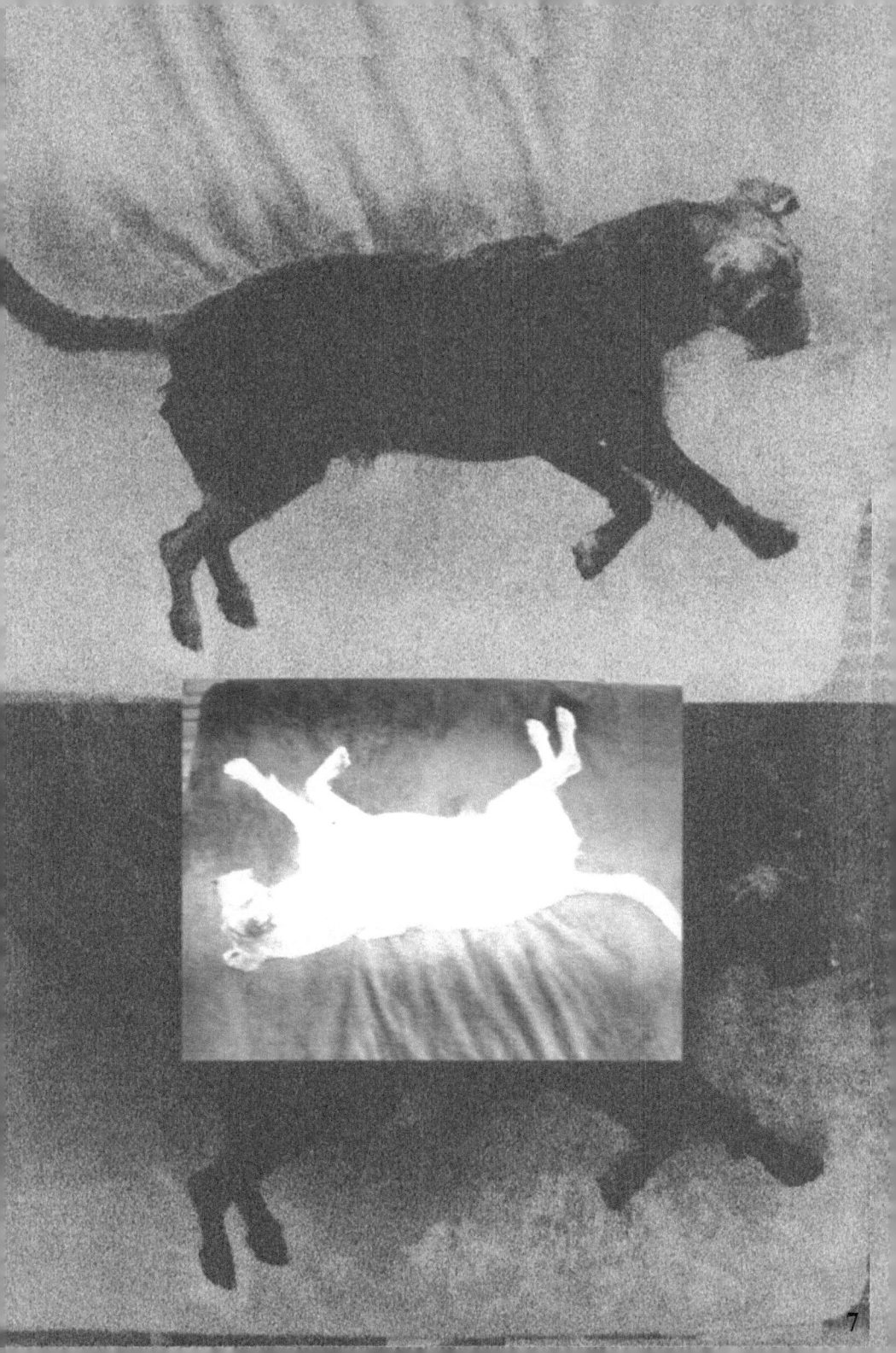

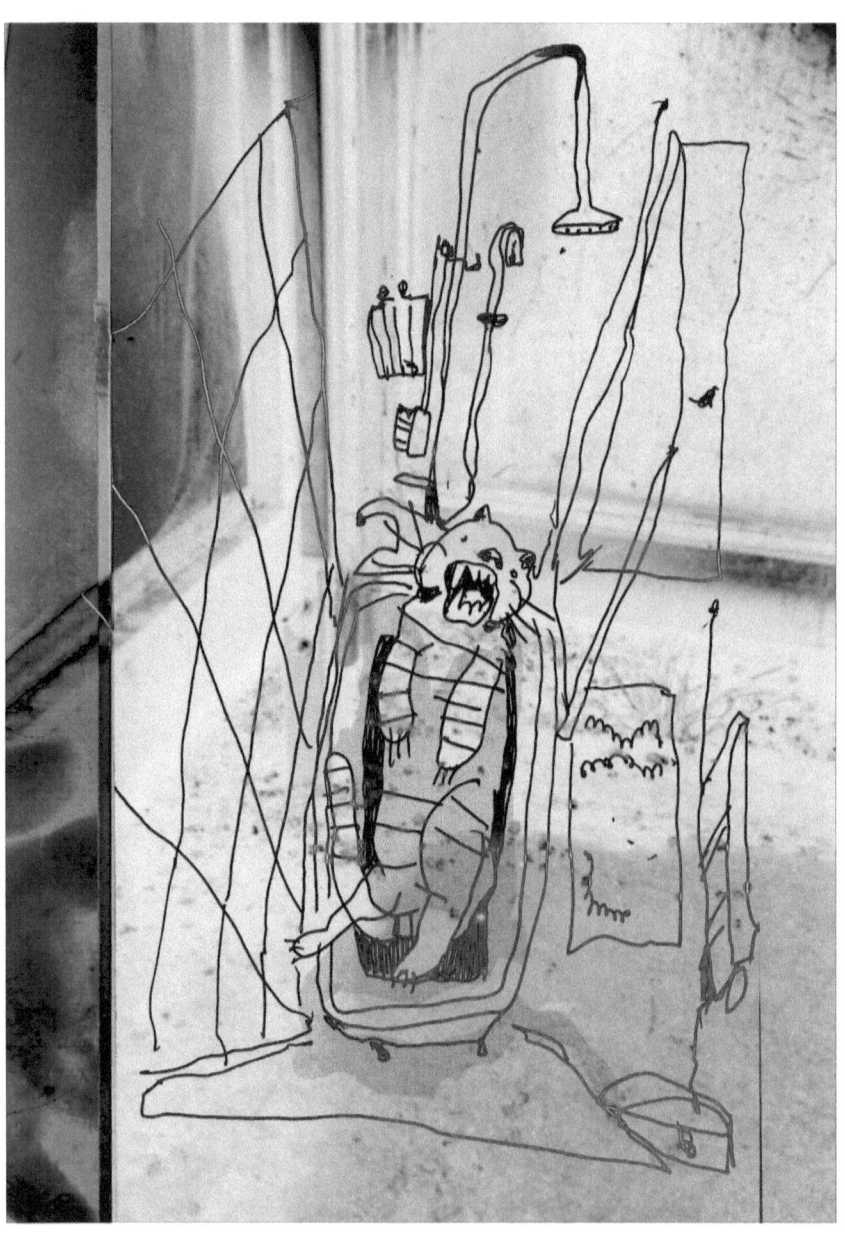

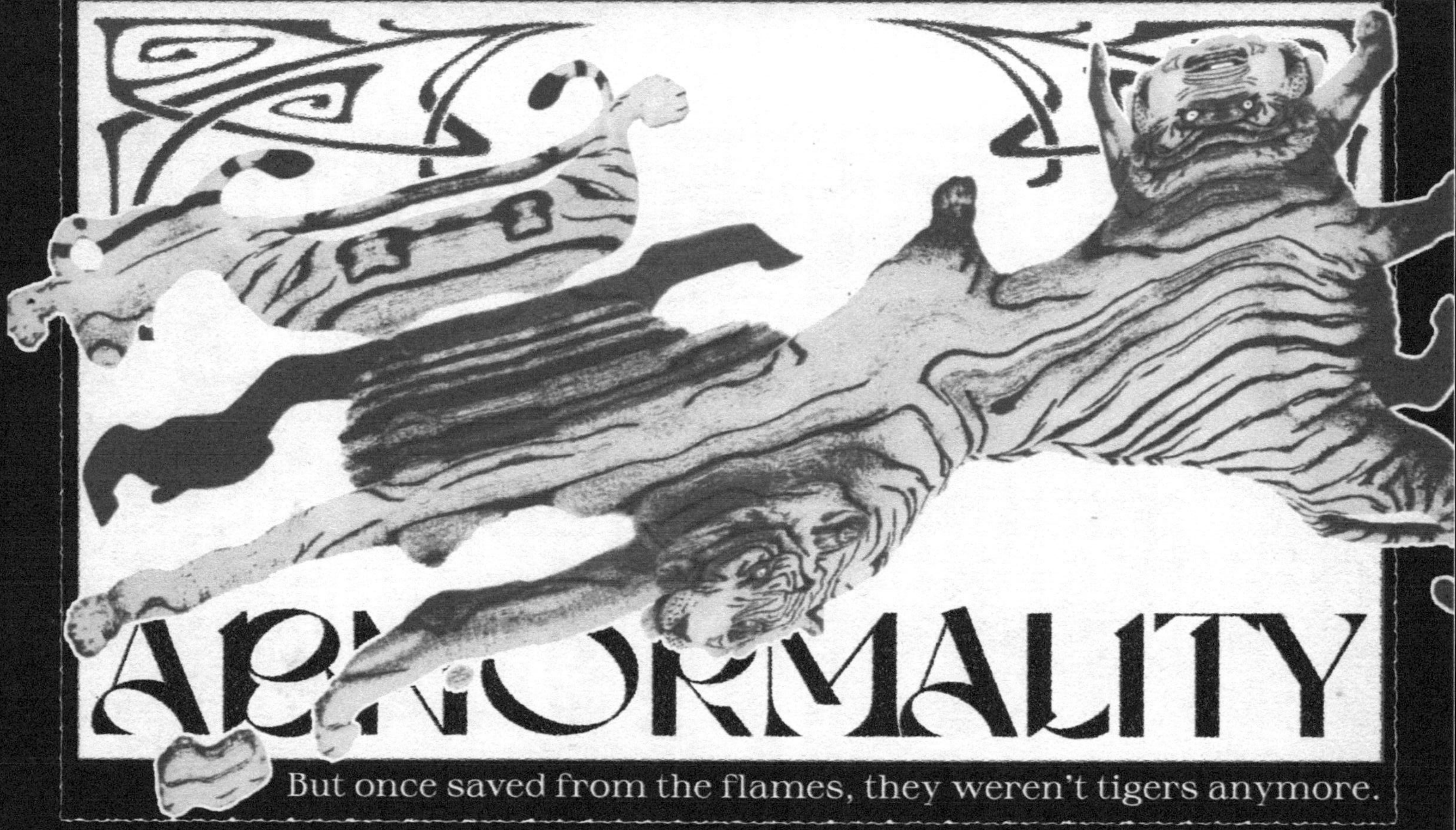

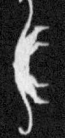

ABNORMALITY

But once saved from the flames, they weren't tigers anymore.

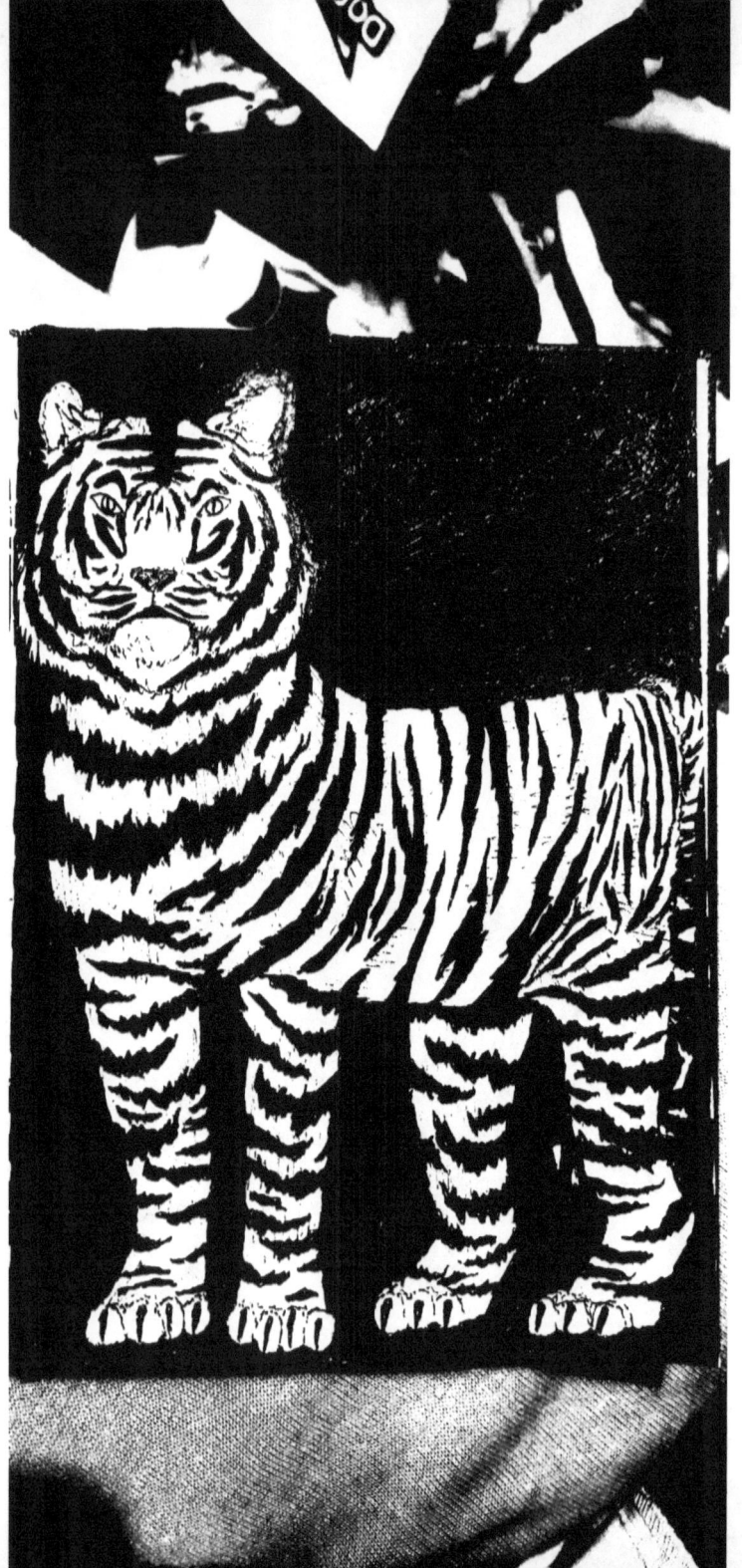

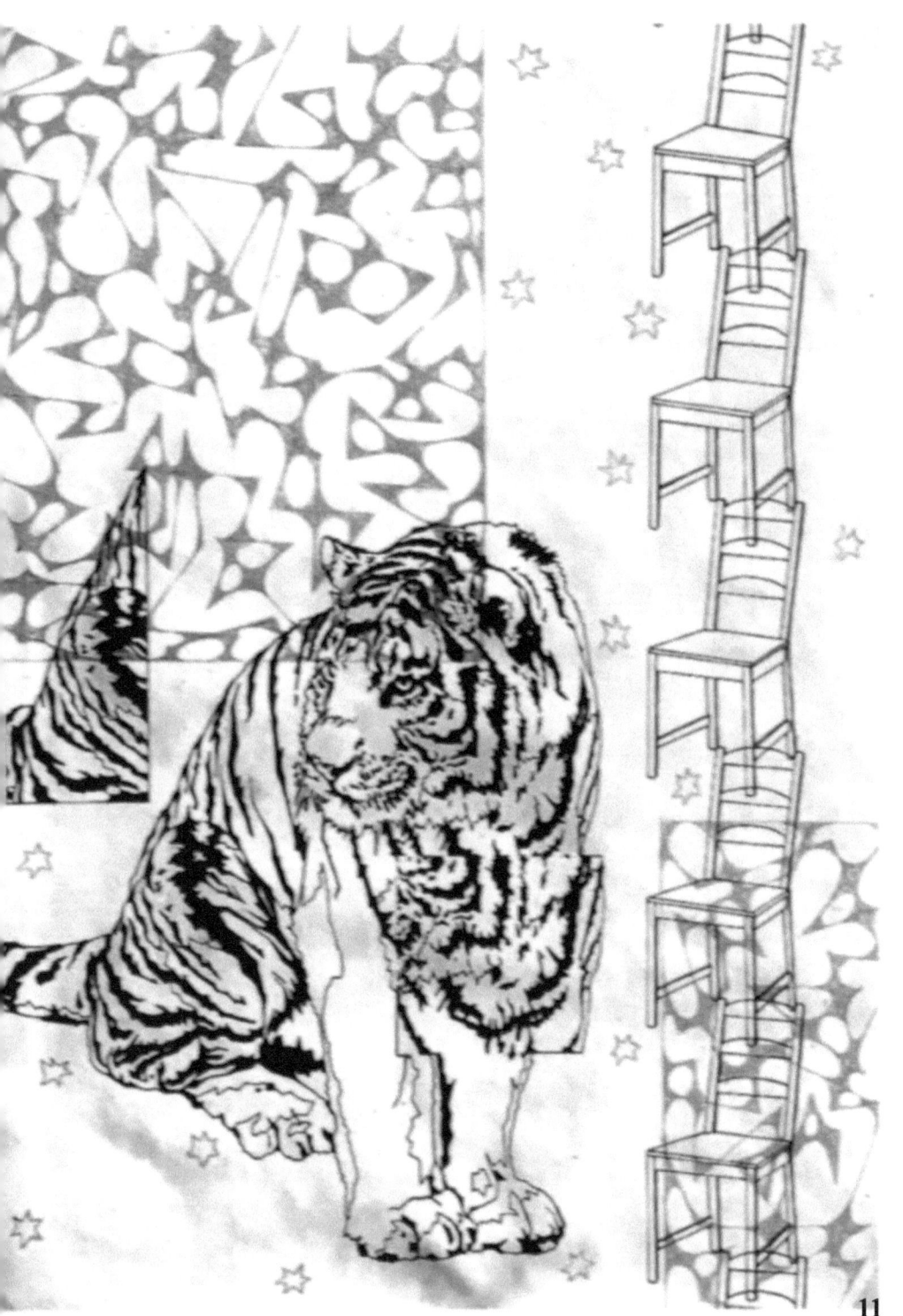

11

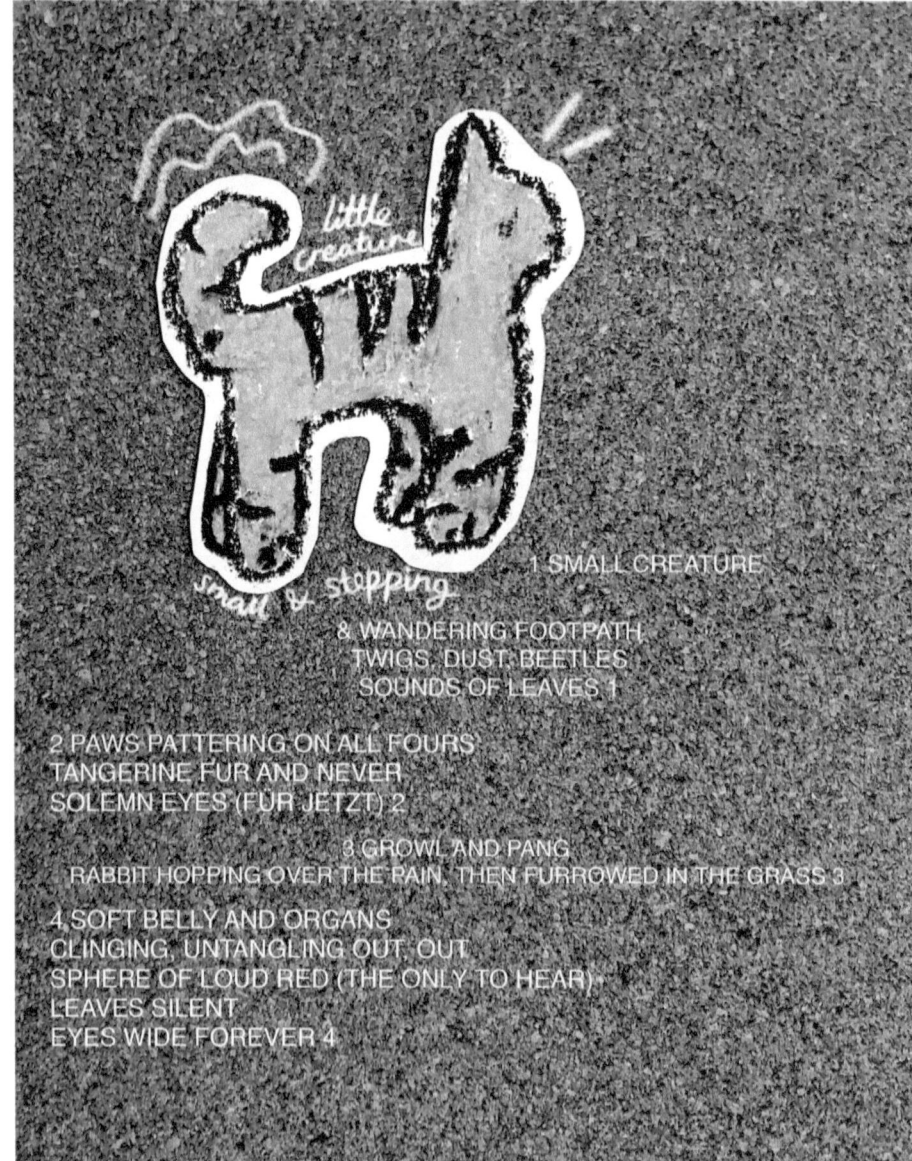

little creature

small & stopping

1 SMALL CREATURE

& WANDERING FOOTPATH
TWIGS, DUST, BEETLES
SOUNDS OF LEAVES 1

2 PAWS PATTERING ON ALL FOURS
TANGERINE FUR AND NEVER
SOLEMN EYES (FÜR JETZT) 2

3 GROWL AND PANG
RABBIT HOPPING OVER THE PAIN, THEN FURROWED IN THE GRASS 3

4 SOFT BELLY AND ORGANS
CLINGING, UNTANGLING OUT, OUT
SPHERE OF LOUD RED (THE ONLY TO HEAR)
LEAVES SILENT
EYES WIDE FOREVER 4

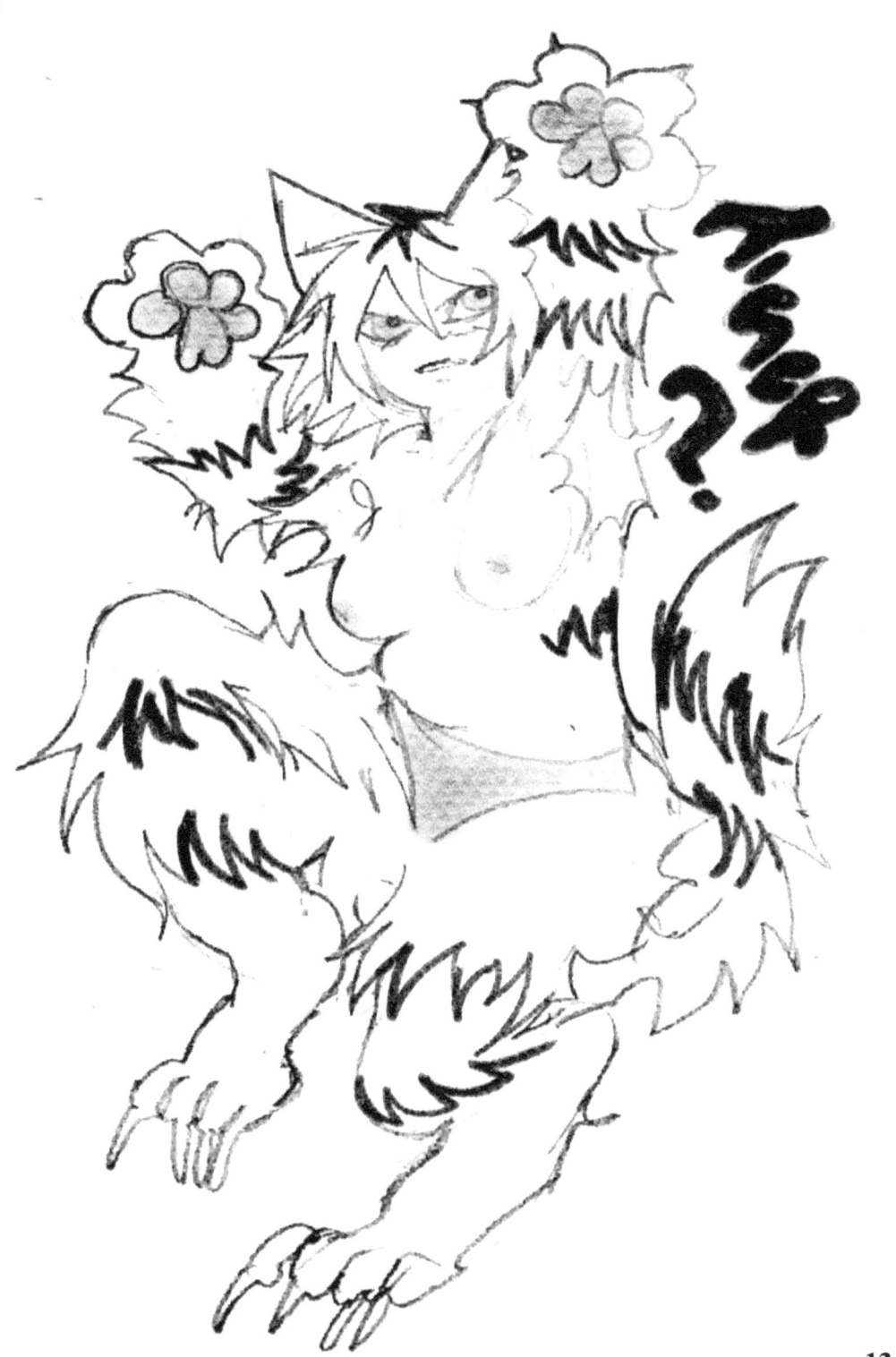

13

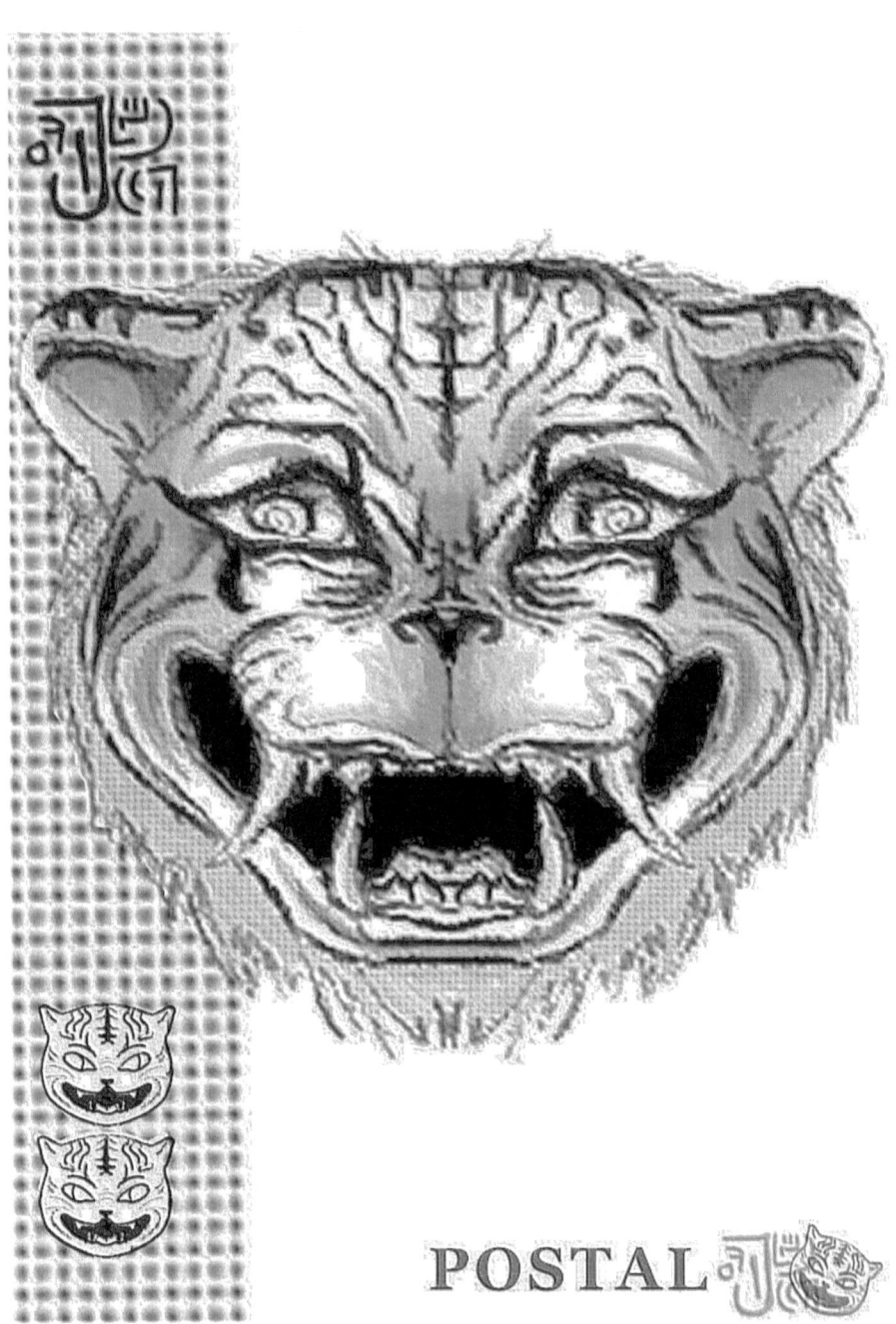

POSTAL

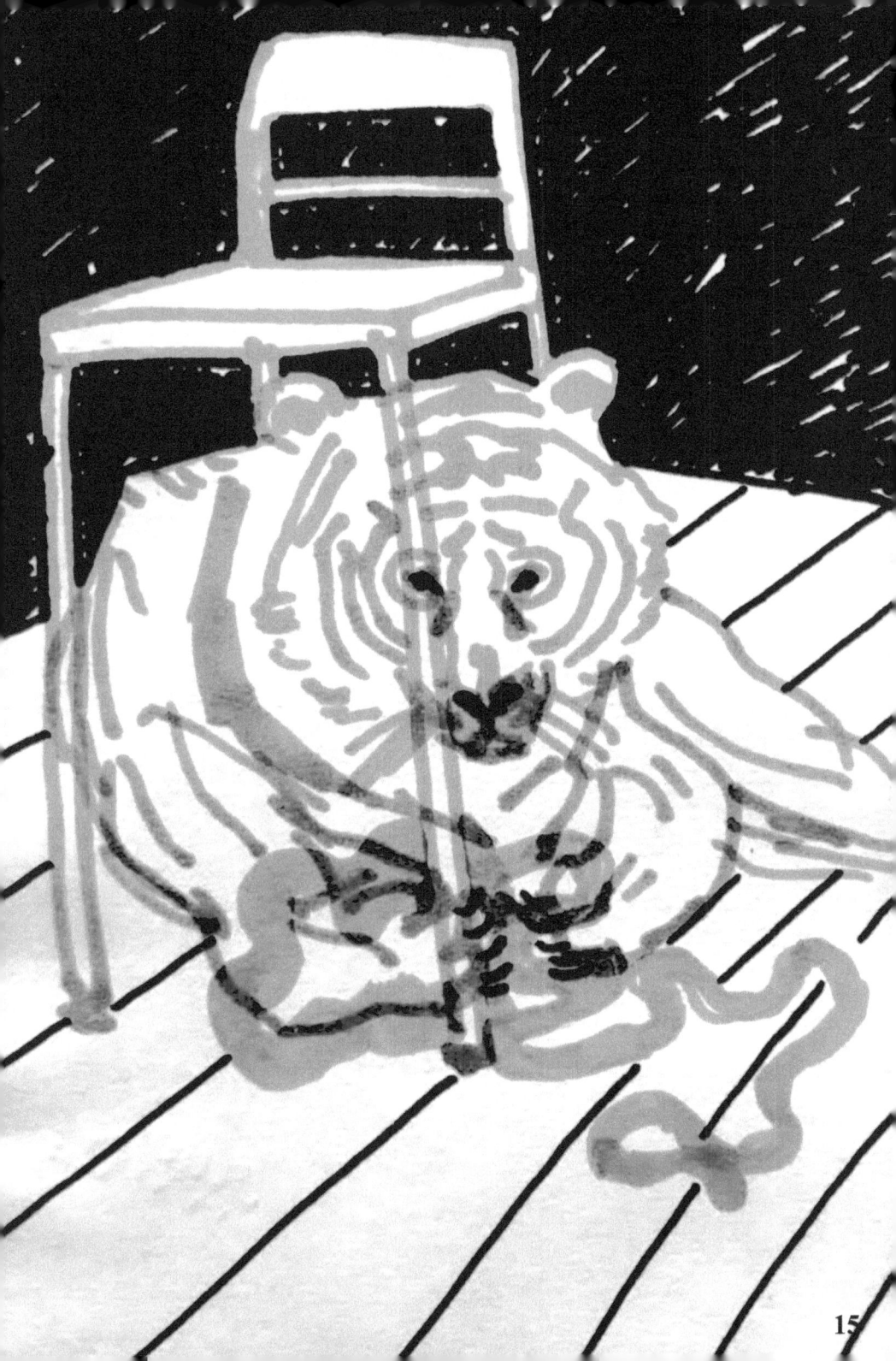

16

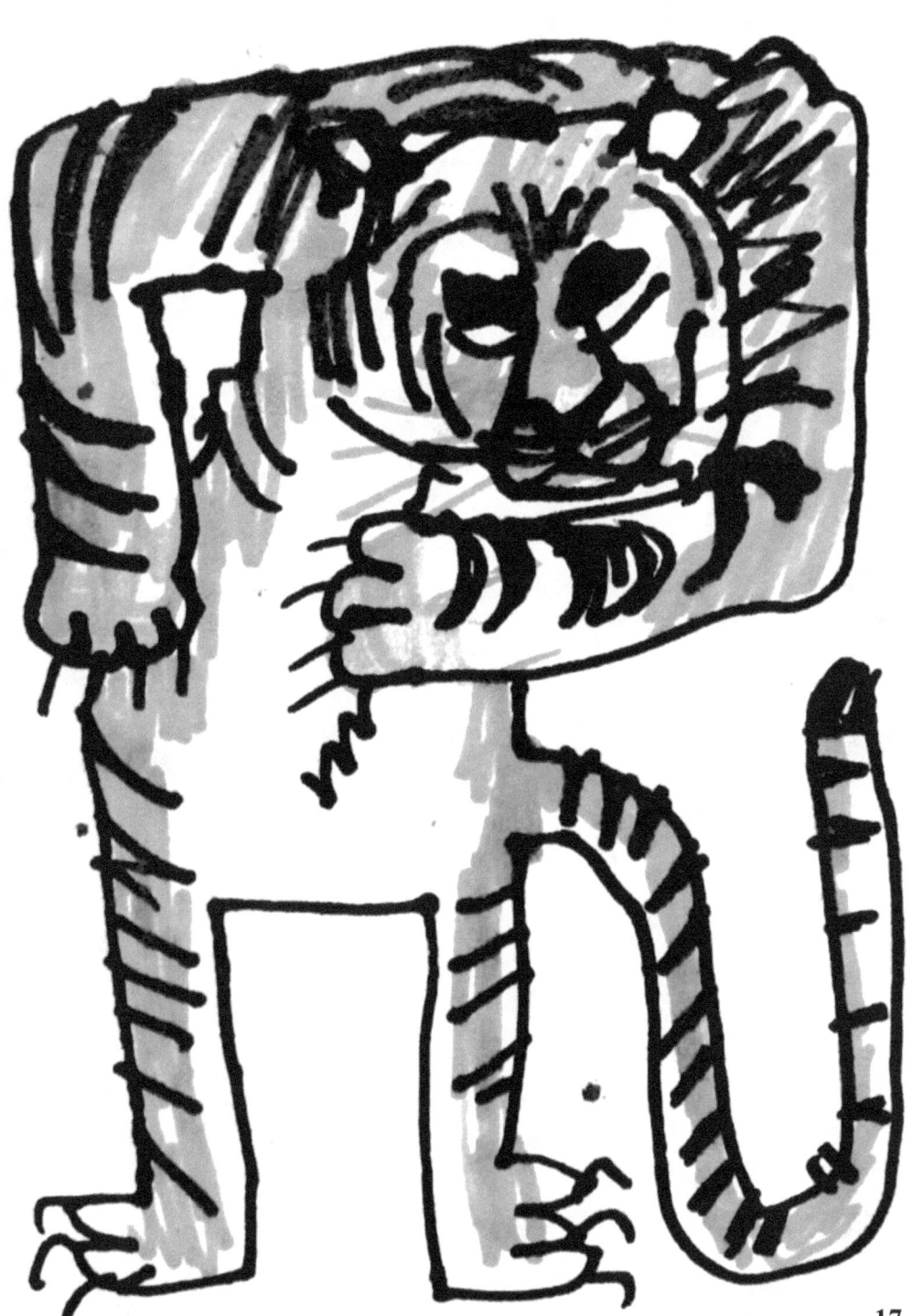

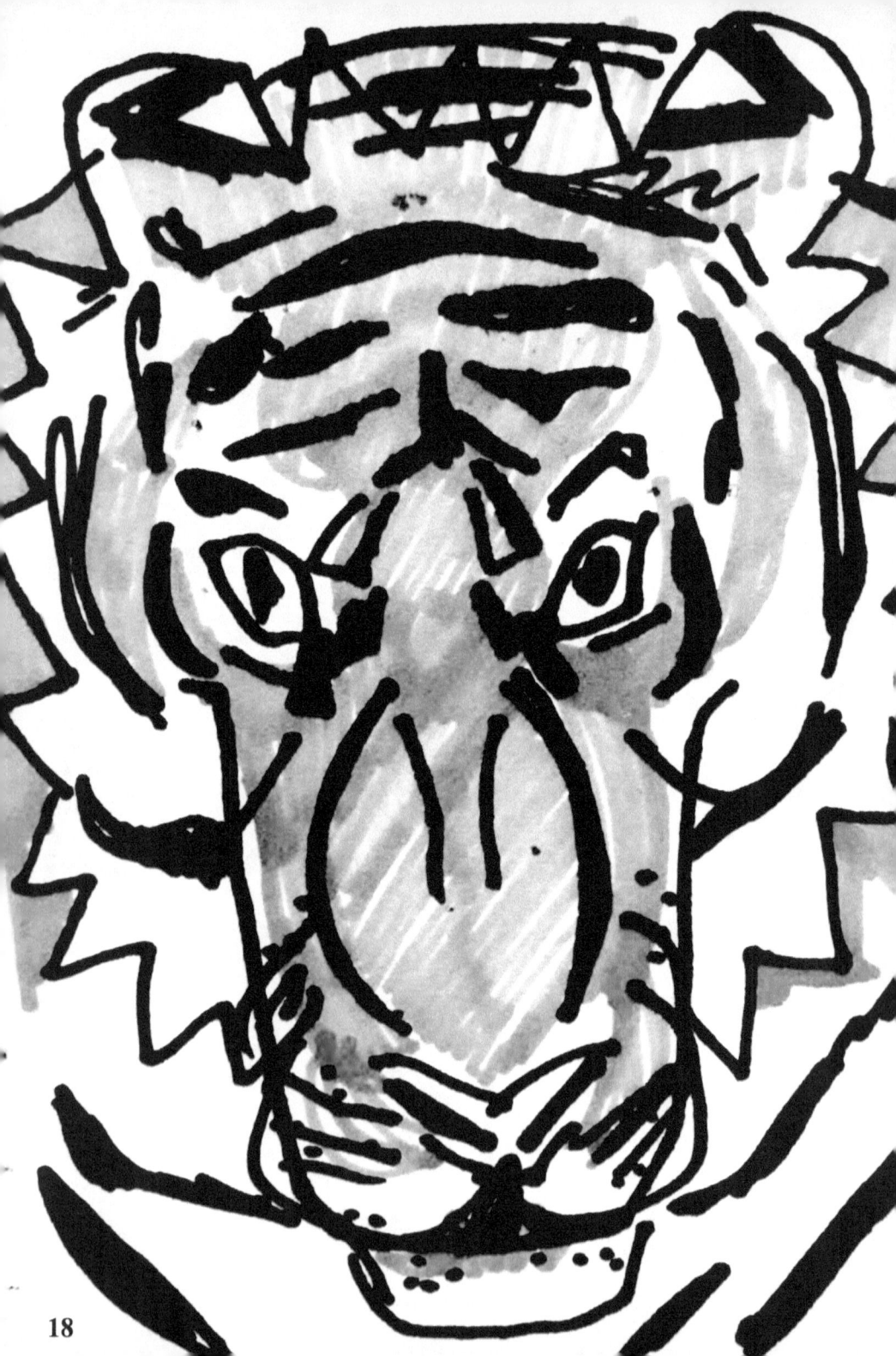

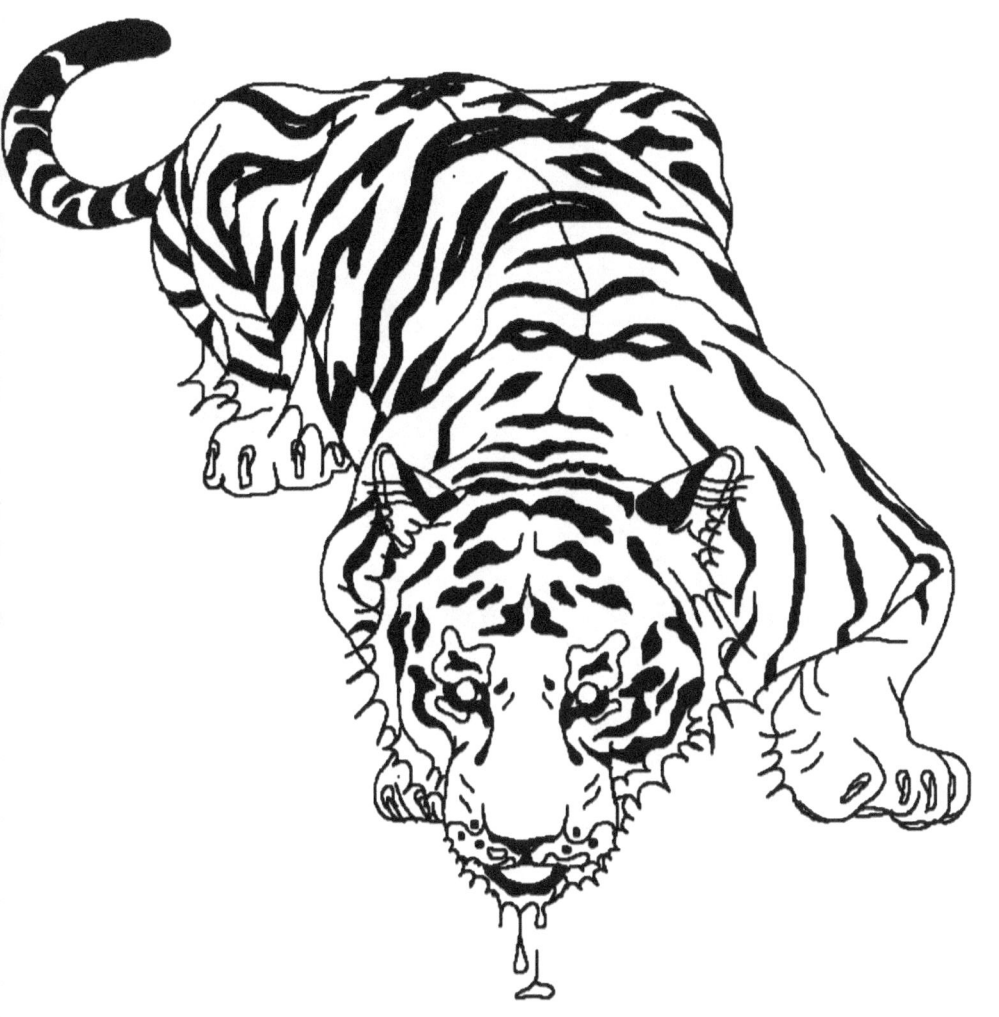

19

호 랑이 (호랑이)

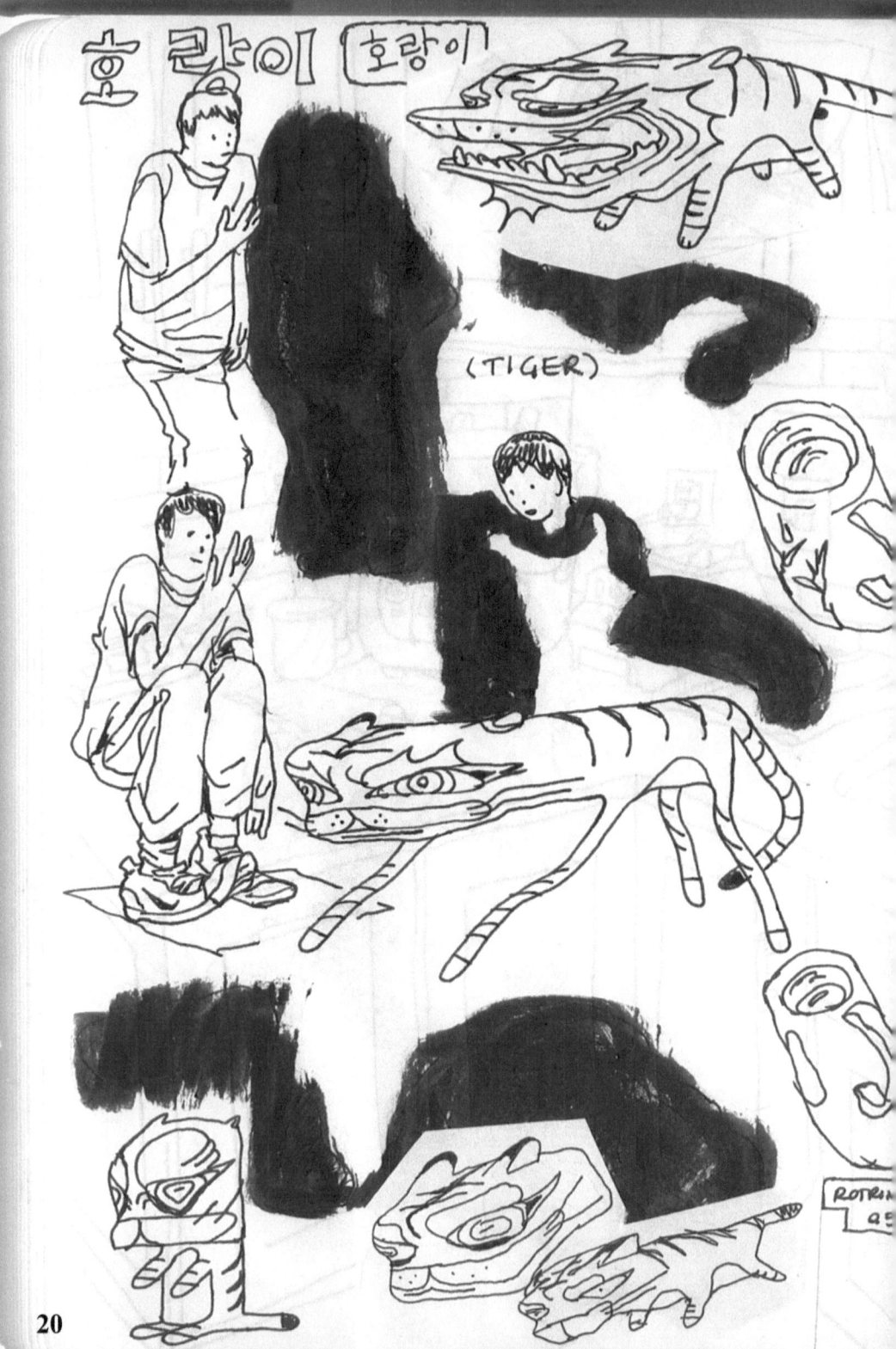

(TIGER)

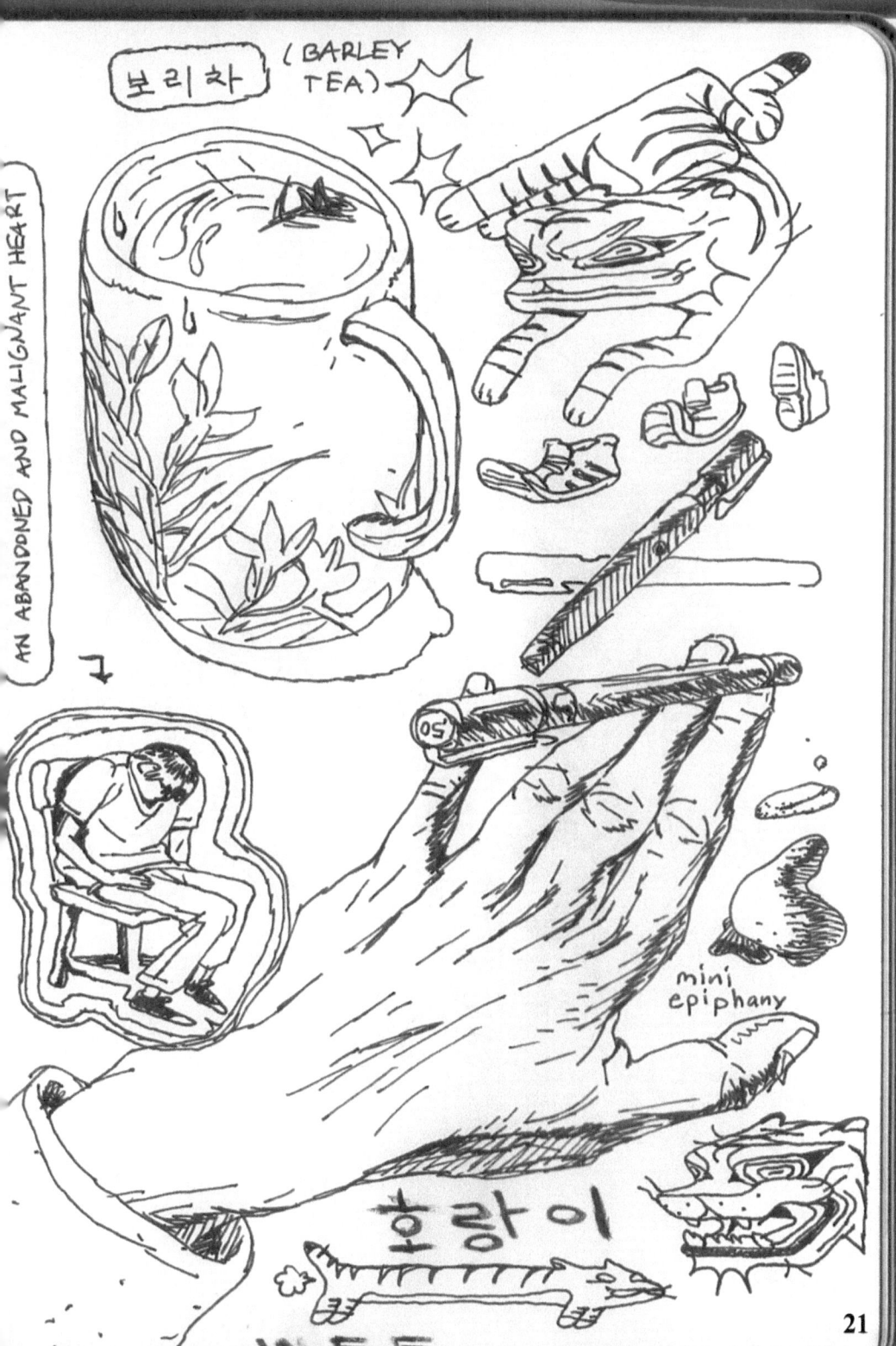

보리차 (BARLEY TEA)

AN ABANDONED AND MALIGNANT HEART

mini epiphany

호랑이

21

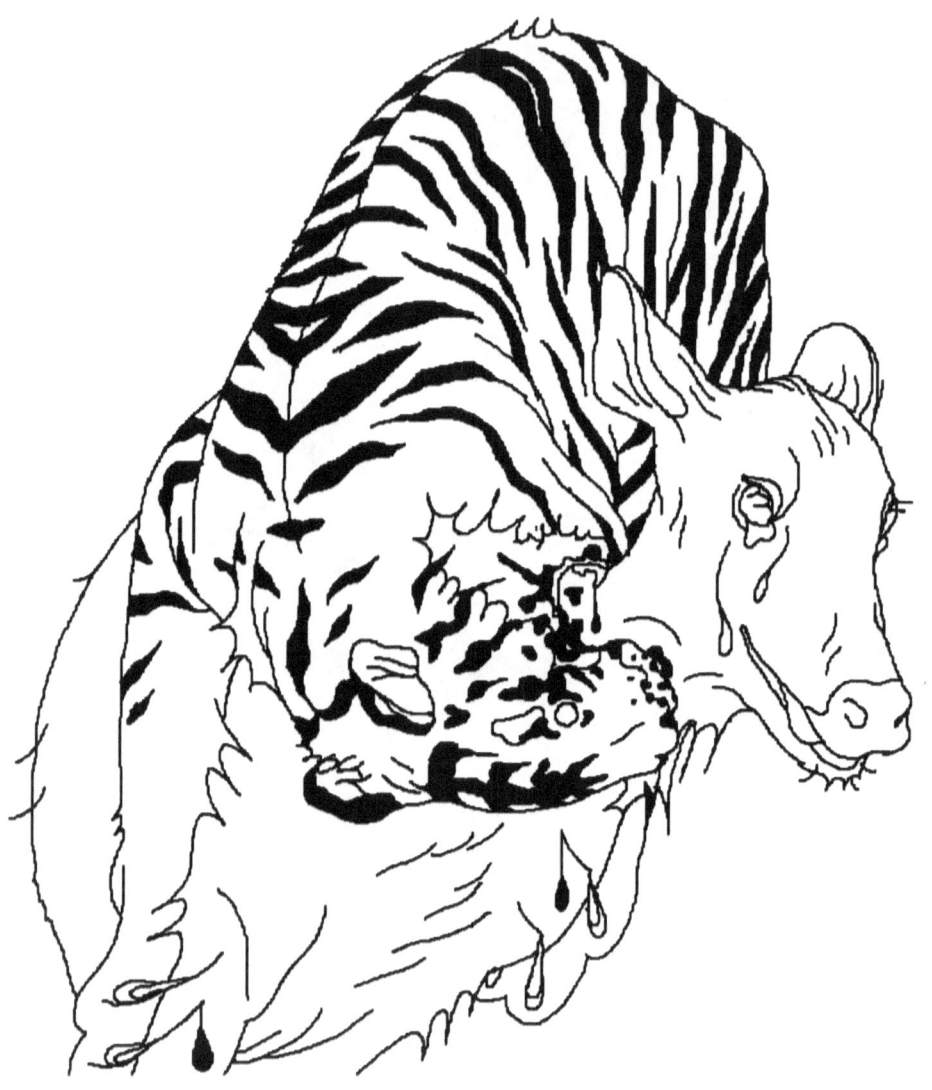

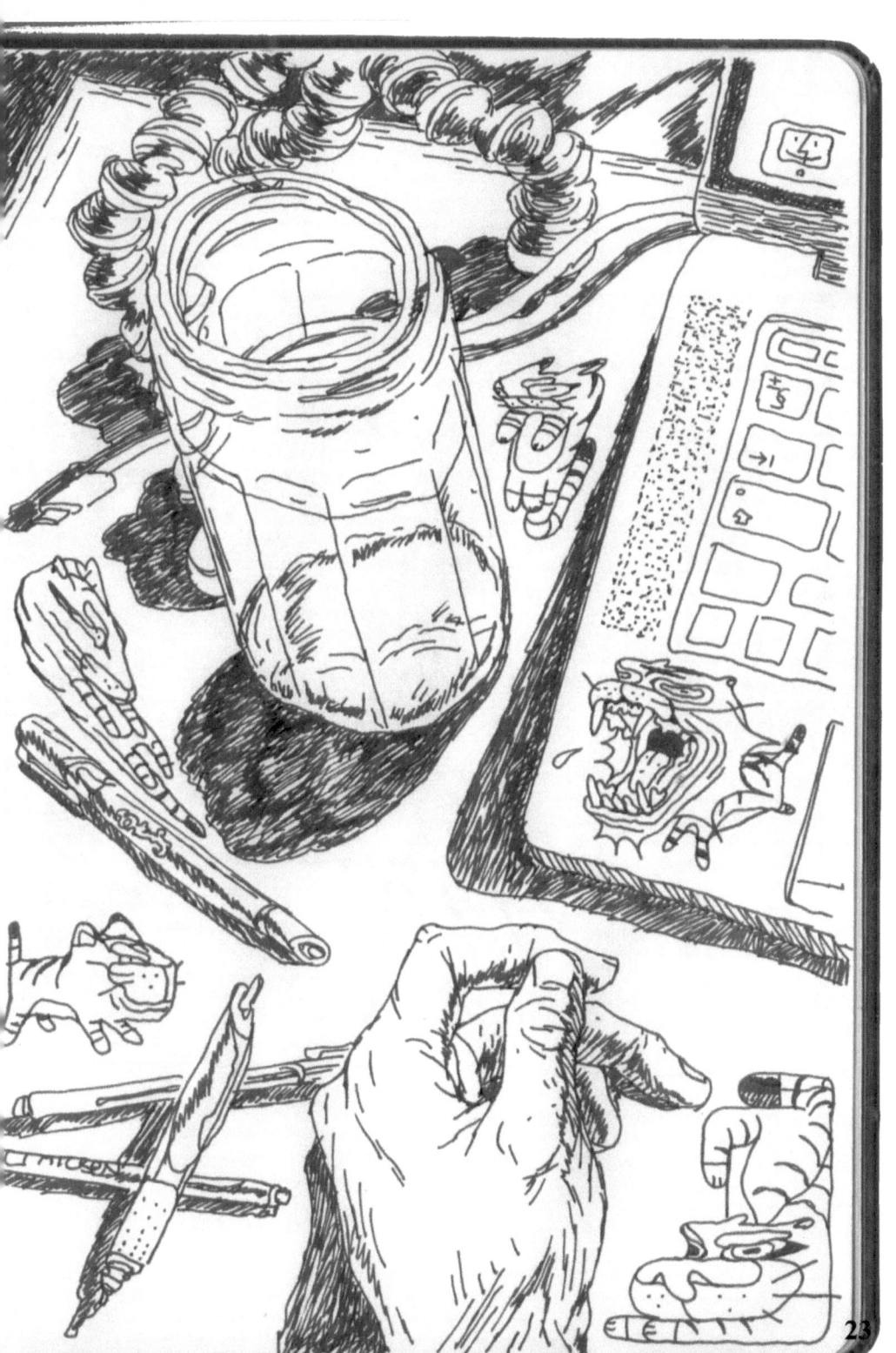

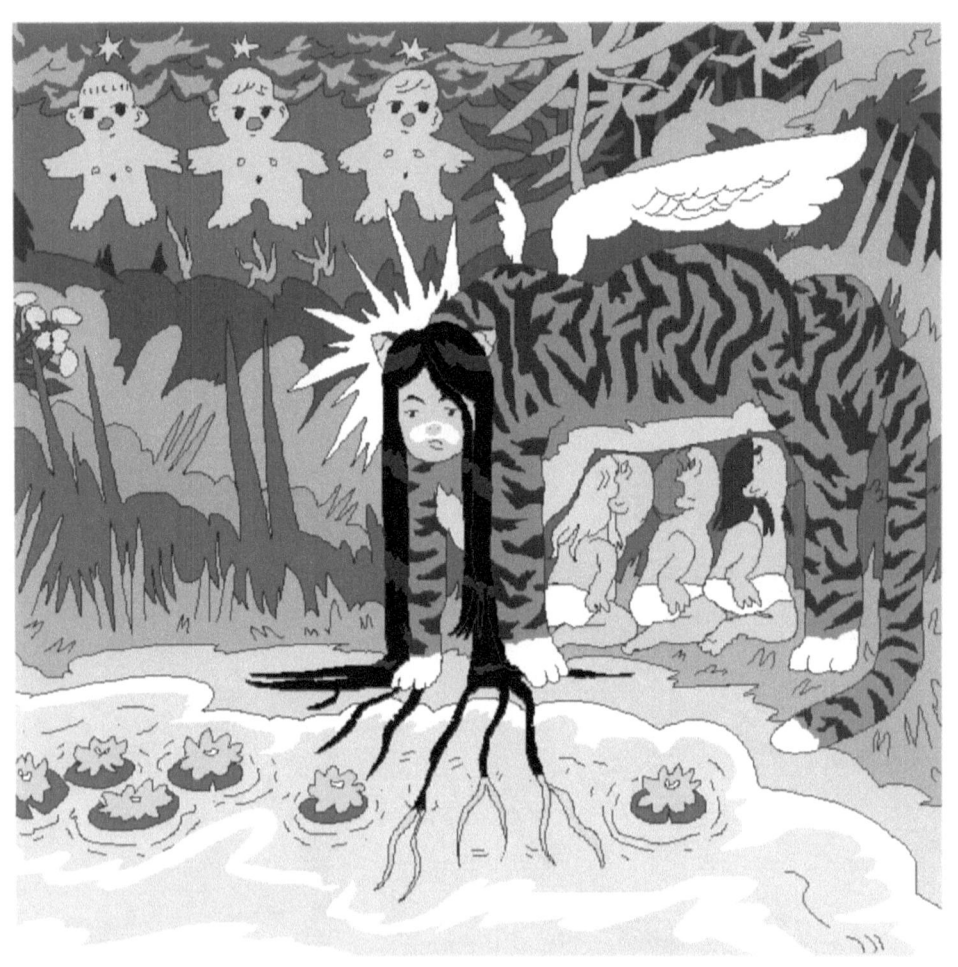

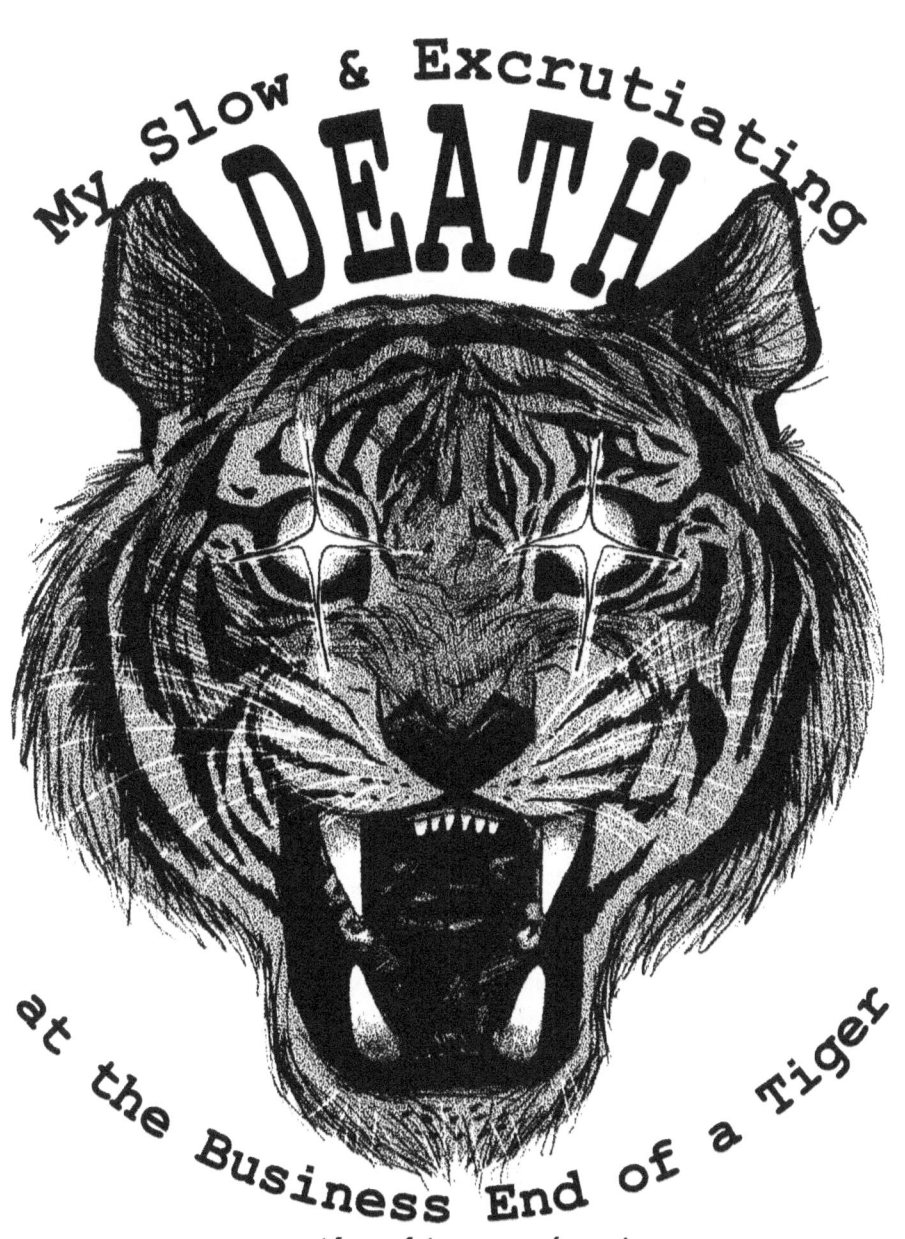

My Slow & Excrutiating DEATH at the Business End of a Tiger

a thought experiment

Perhaps the sinking feeling in my guts is more
than only the summation of my daily anxieties.
Perhaps I am being pursued by a hungry tiger. Am
I only hearing things or is there gentle
breathing that is not mine?

Maybe I am stalked for good reason and
not only for sport. She has hungry cubs
whose stomachs roil with anticipation
of a next meal. She is so much stronger
than me - I haven't the hope to stand
a chance against her savage paws and
vicious teeth. If I only sit still long
enough, she will pounce.

All she has to do is find her mouth around
my neck and bite. My spine would sever,
my arteries would spew, my windpipe
collapse. I would be dead in seconds.

Would that I could be the pounds of
flesh her babes long to gorge
themselves on. Would that I could
be the blood on their muzzles and
the strength in their legs, if only
to be fuel to the fire in
their eyes.

I could slough off the pieces of
myself that languish and suffer,
fearing death and her ever closing proximity,
encroaching upon me. That stubborn part of me
could be spirited away and persist, hunting
and fighting to the last - that part of me
that so wishes for death *and* glory.

Who's to say it's not possible?

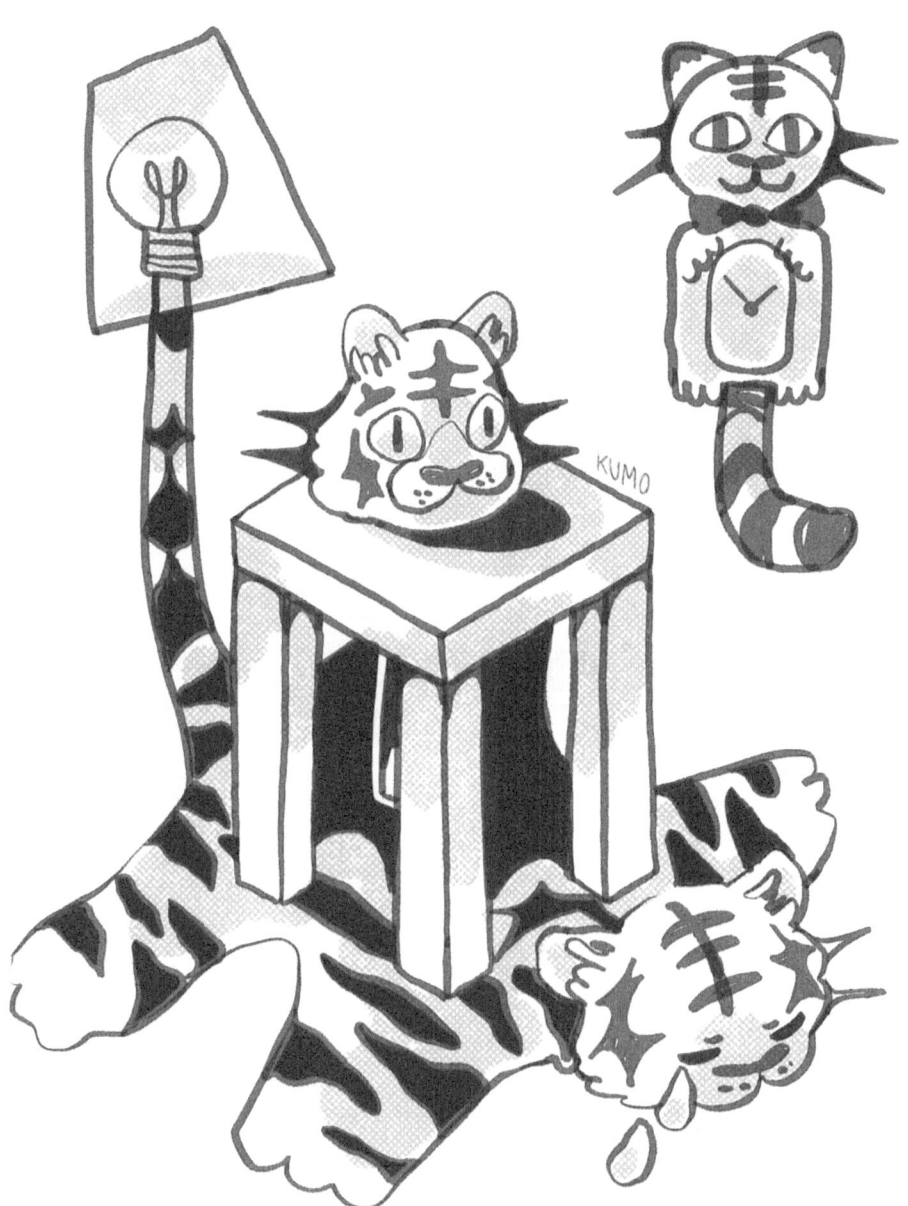

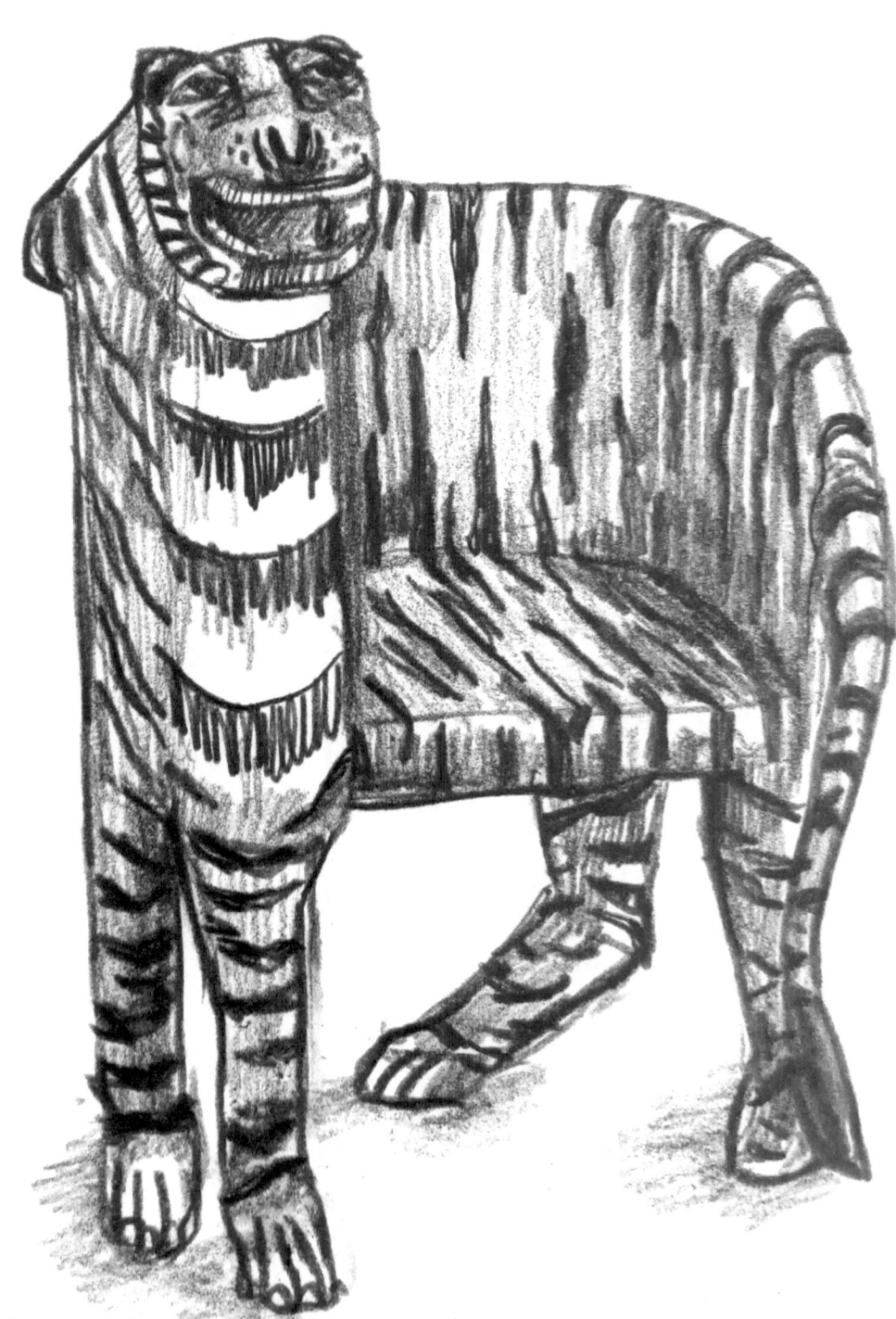

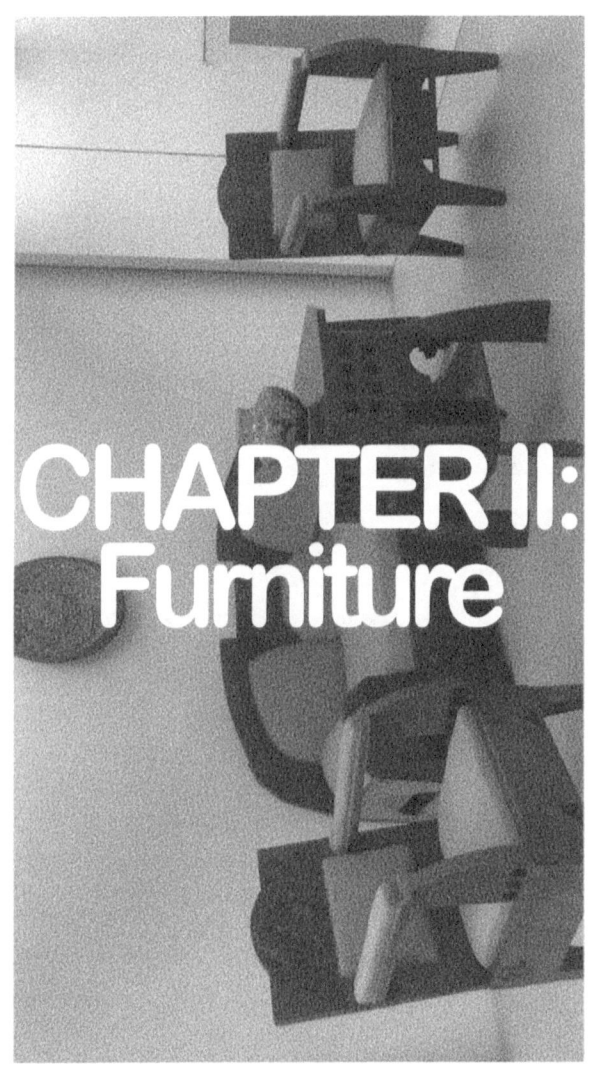

CHAPTER II:
Furniture

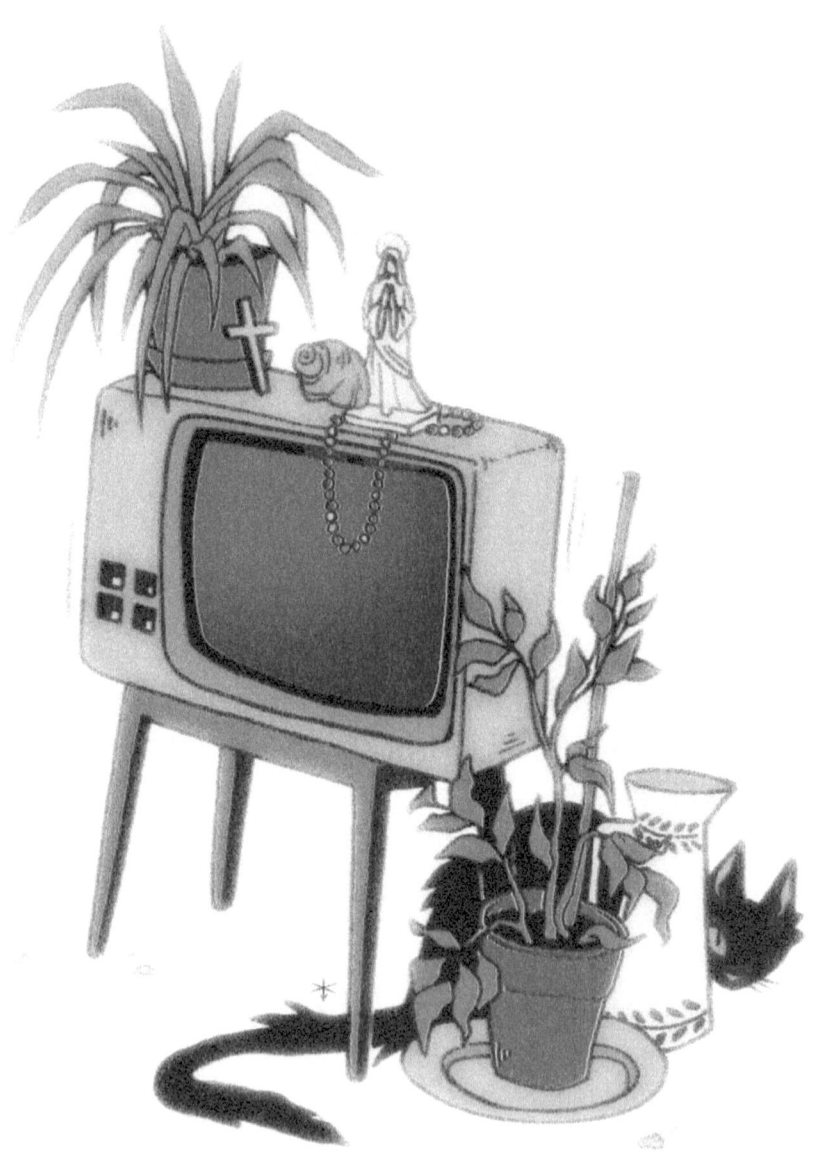

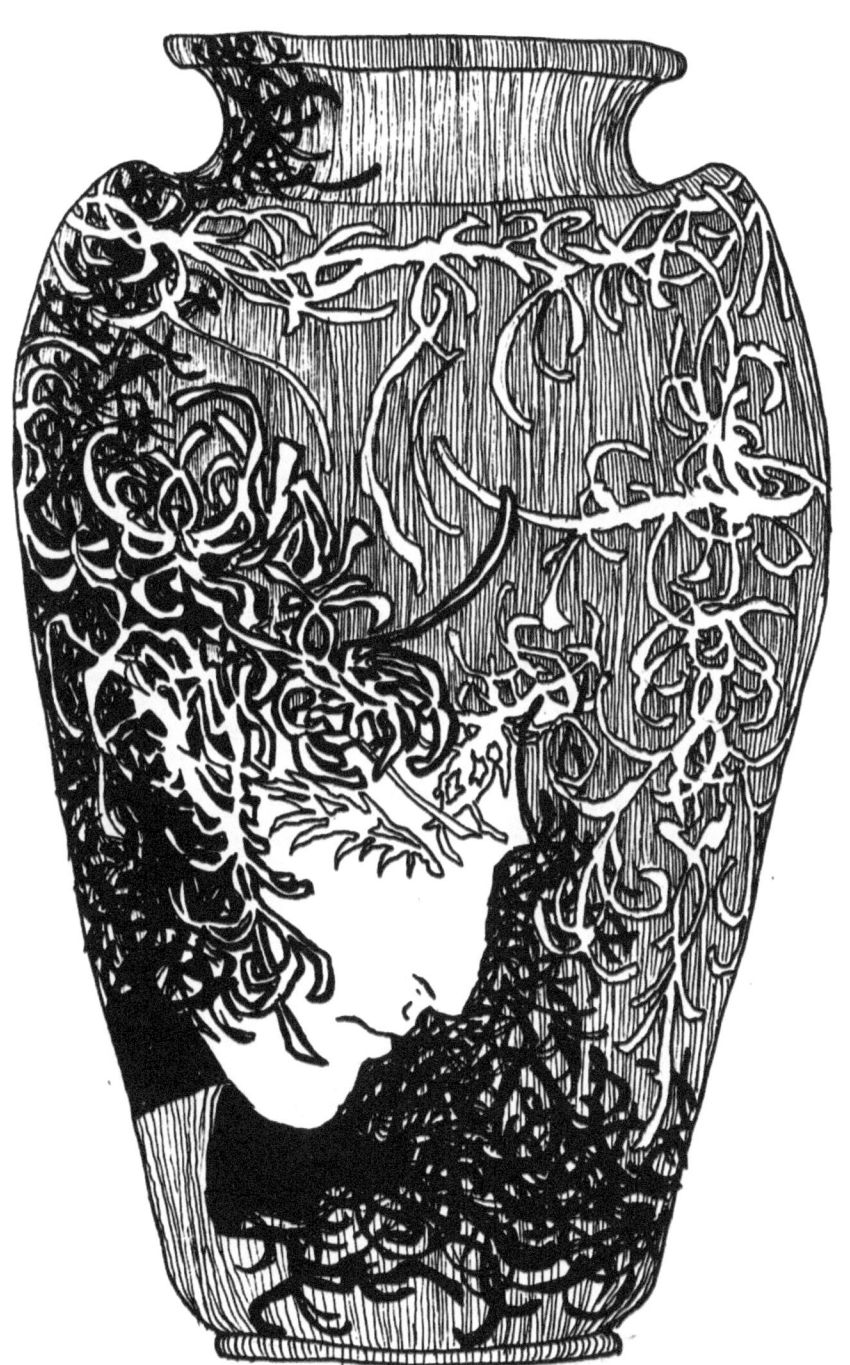

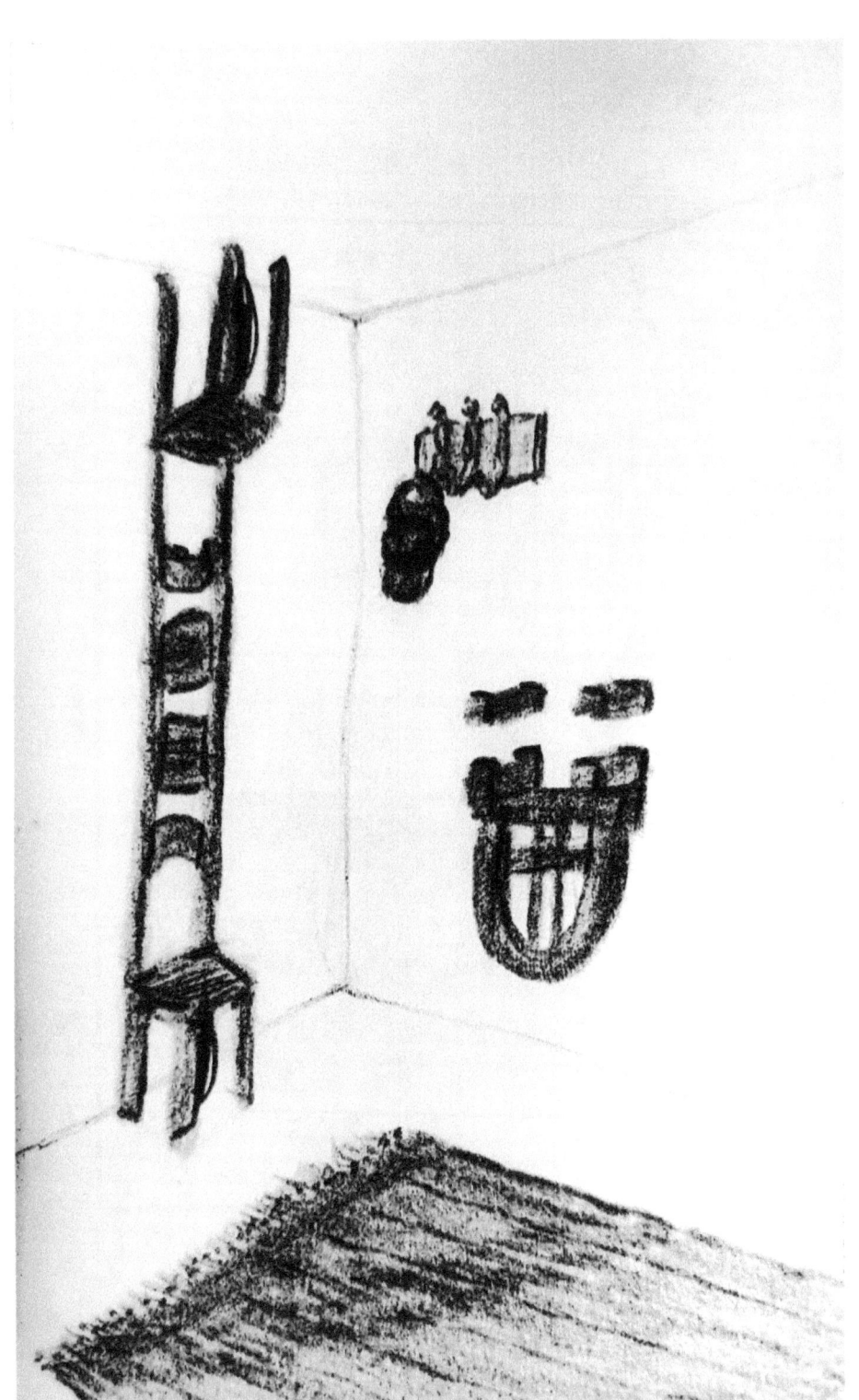

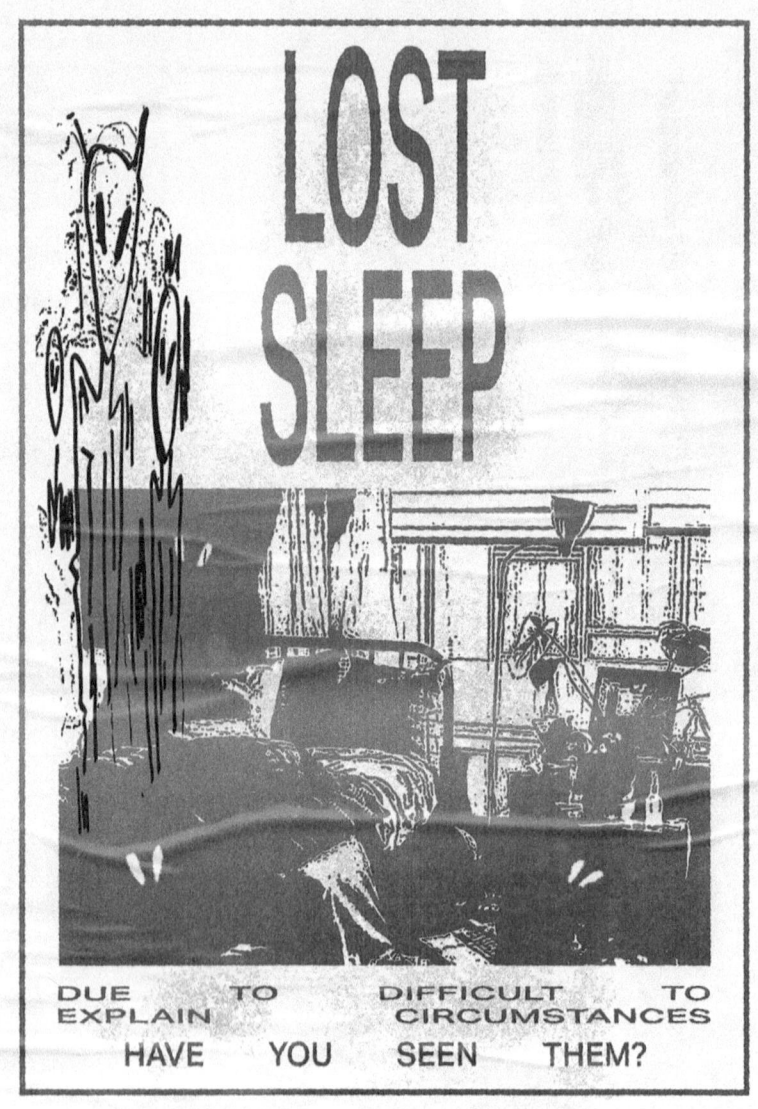

SUGAR BEE HONEY JACKET

There's a hornet bored into the maple stump
A bumble bee's head on my windowsill
                                    Our furniture used to be
someone else's
Before the middles were missing
Who will recane this framework?
I watch videos on the importance of skill
How the country is slave to sweets
I am trying to eat less sugar
We are all trying to eat less sugar.

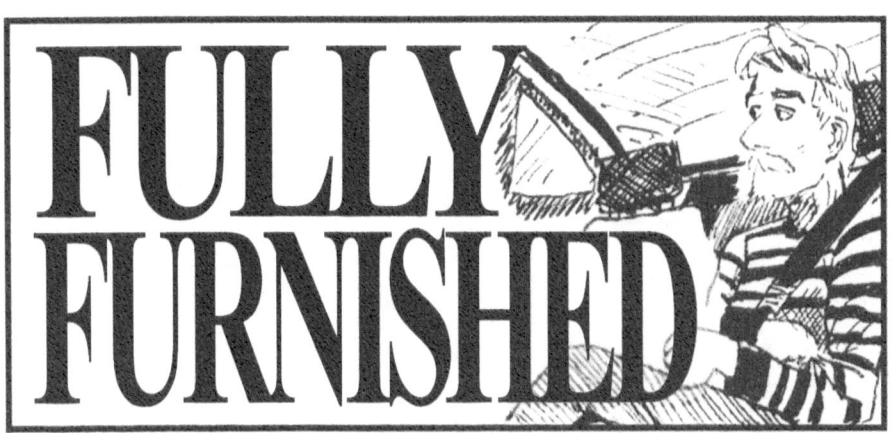

FULLY FURNISHED

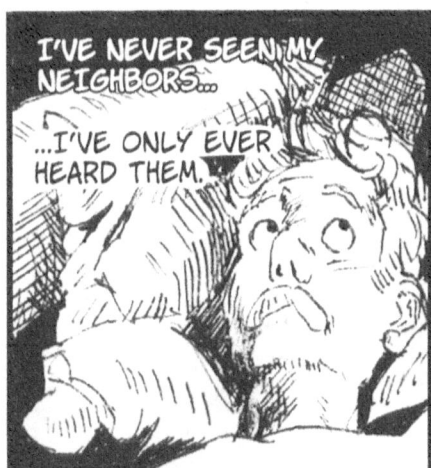

I'VE NEVER SEEN MY NEIGHBORS...

...I'VE ONLY EVER HEARD THEM.

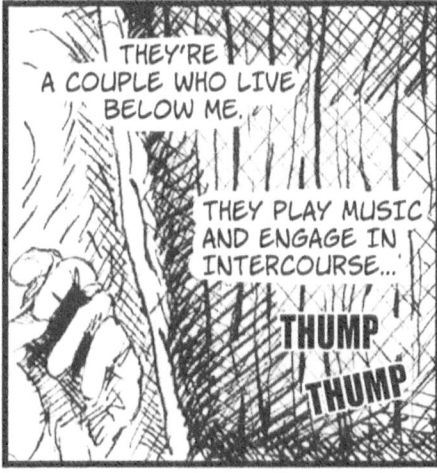

THEY'RE A COUPLE WHO LIVE BELOW ME.

THEY PLAY MUSIC AND ENGAGE IN INTERCOURSE...

THUMP

THUMP

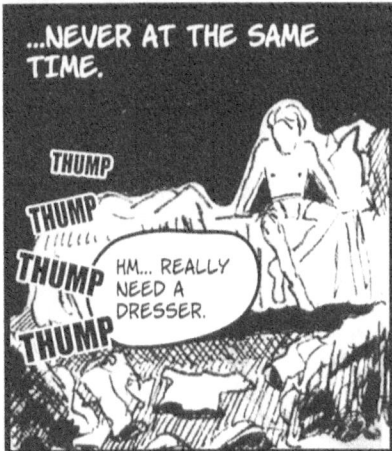

...NEVER AT THE SAME TIME.

THUMP

THUMP

THUMP

THUMP

HM... REALLY NEED A DRESSER.

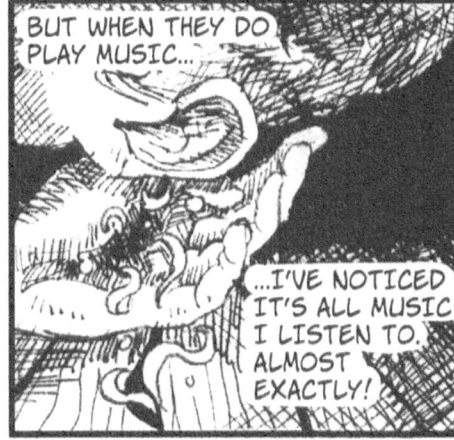

BUT WHEN THEY DO PLAY MUSIC...

...I'VE NOTICED IT'S ALL MUSIC I LISTEN TO. ALMOST EXACTLY!

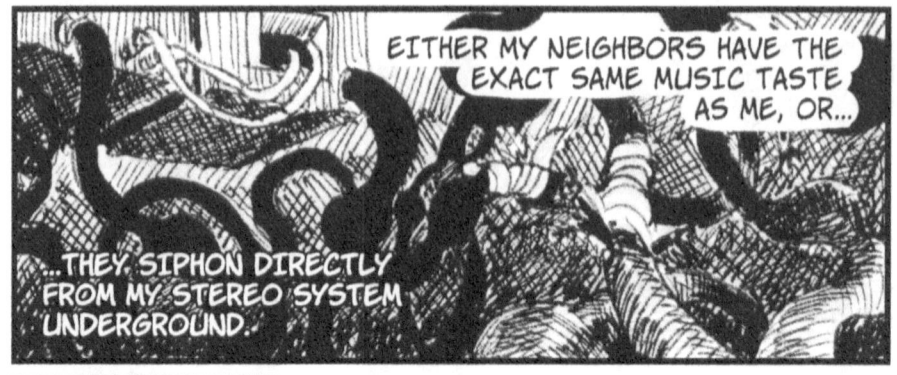

EITHER MY NEIGHBORS HAVE THE EXACT SAME MUSIC TASTE AS ME, OR...

...THEY SIPHON DIRECTLY FROM MY STEREO SYSTEM UNDERGROUND.

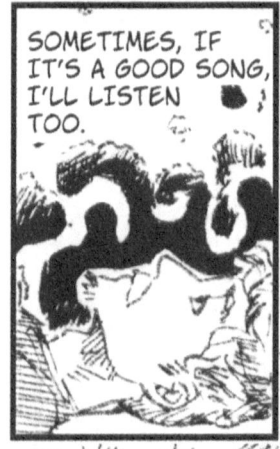

SOMETIMES, IF IT'S A GOOD SONG, I'LL LISTEN TOO.

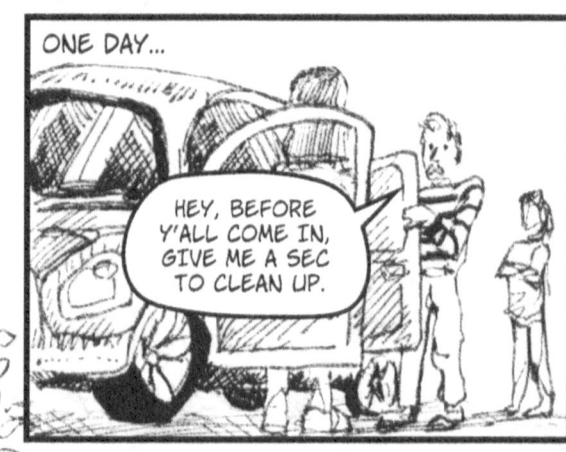

ONE DAY...

HEY, BEFORE Y'ALL COME IN, GIVE ME A SEC TO CLEAN UP.

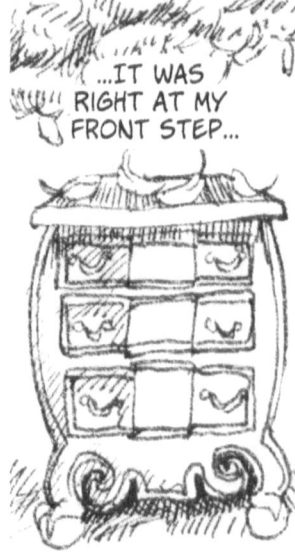

...IT WAS RIGHT AT MY FRONT STEP...

...LIKE AN ANSWERED PRAYER.

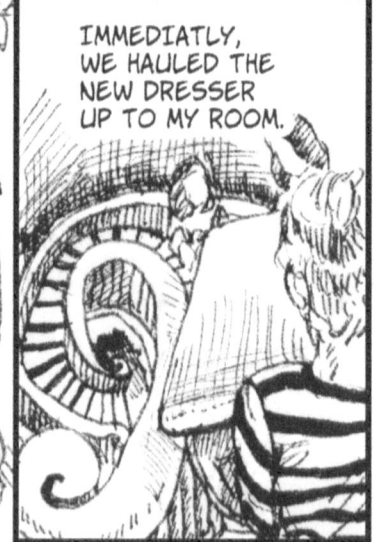

IMMEDIATLY, WE HAULED THE NEW DRESSER UP TO MY ROOM.

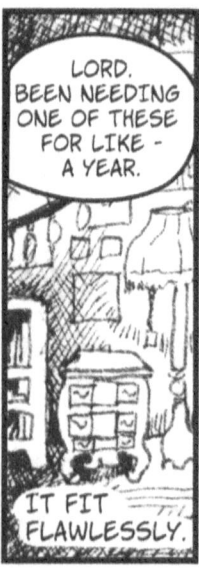

LORD. BEEN NEEDING ONE OF THESE FOR LIKE - A YEAR.

IT FIT FLAWLESSLY.

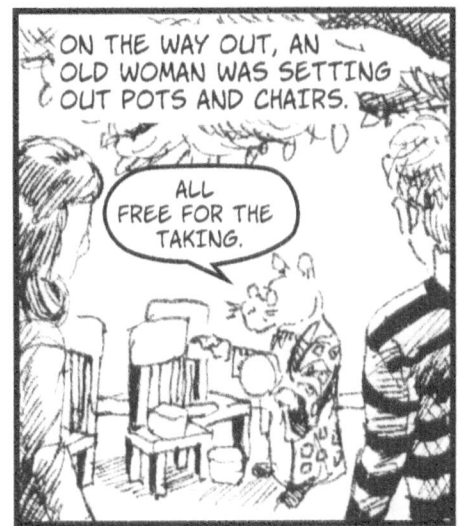

ON THE WAY OUT, AN OLD WOMAN WAS SETTING OUT POTS AND CHAIRS.

ALL FREE FOR THE TAKING.

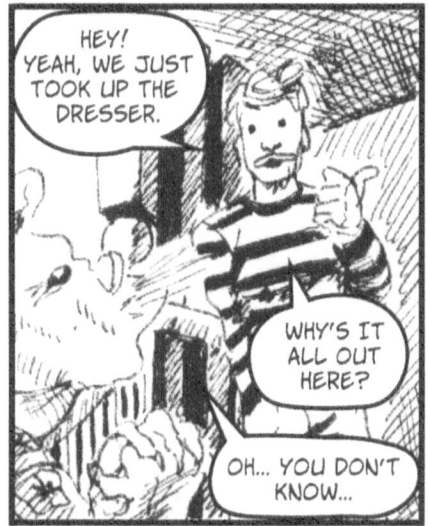

HEY! YEAH, WE JUST TOOK UP THE DRESSER.

WHY'S IT ALL OUT HERE?

OH... YOU DON'T KNOW...

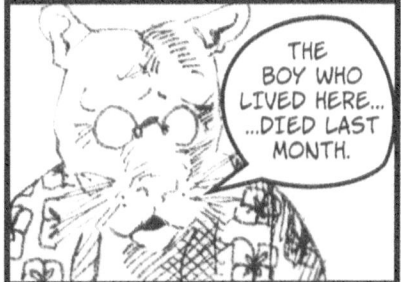

THE BOY WHO LIVED HERE... ...DIED LAST MONTH.

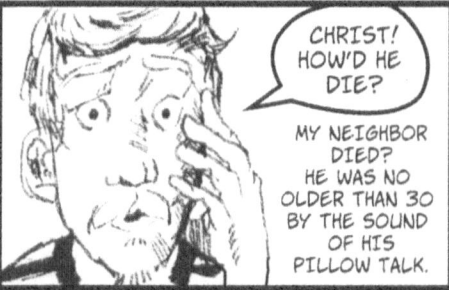

CHRIST! HOW'D HE DIE?

MY NEIGHBOR DIED? HE WAS NO OLDER THAN 30 BY THE SOUND OF HIS PILLOW TALK.

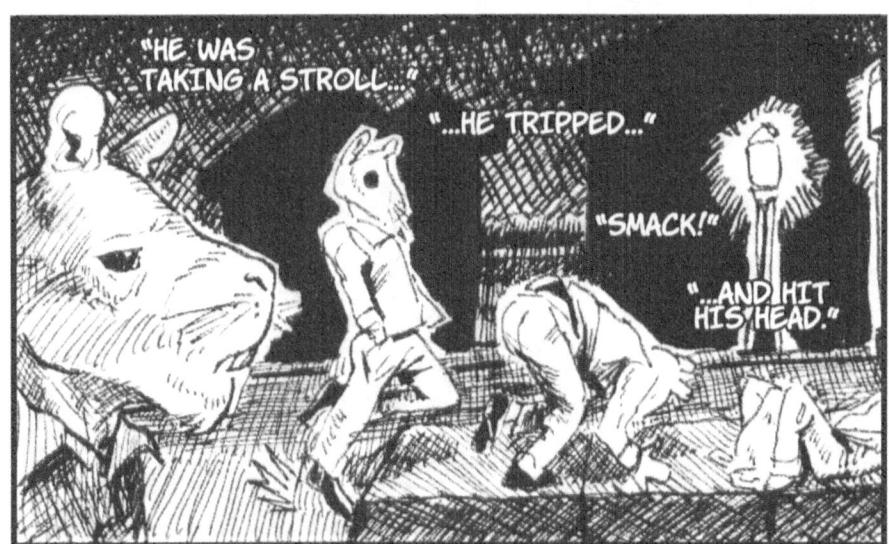

"HE WAS TAKING A STROLL..."

"...HE TRIPPED..."

"SMACK!"

"...AND HIT HIS HEAD."

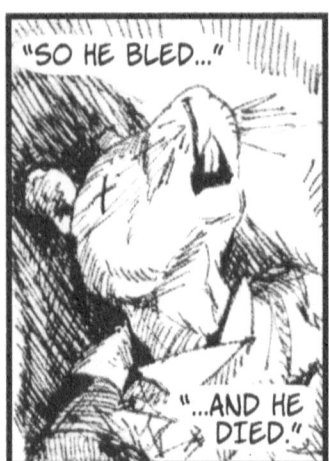

"SO HE BLED..."

"...AND HE DIED."

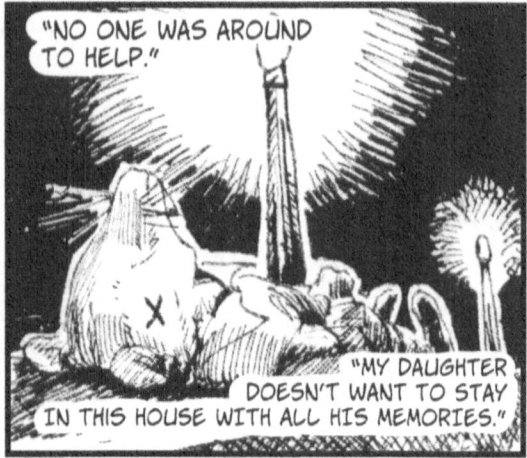

"NO ONE WAS AROUND TO HELP."

"MY DAUGHTER DOESN'T WANT TO STAY IN THIS HOUSE WITH ALL HIS MEMORIES."

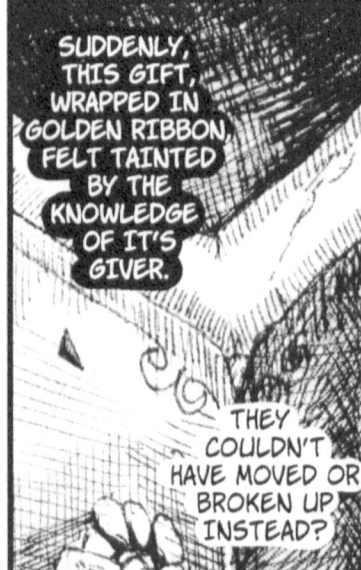

SUDDENLY, THIS GIFT, WRAPPED IN GOLDEN RIBBON, FELT TAINTED BY THE KNOWLEDGE OF IT'S GIVER.

THEY COULDN'T HAVE MOVED OR BROKEN UP INSTEAD?

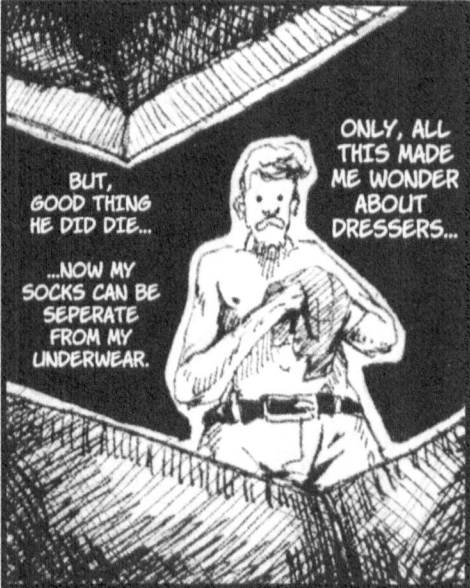

BUT, GOOD THING HE DID DIE...

...NOW MY SOCKS CAN BE SEPERATE FROM MY UNDERWEAR.

ONLY, ALL THIS MADE ME WONDER ABOUT DRESSERS...

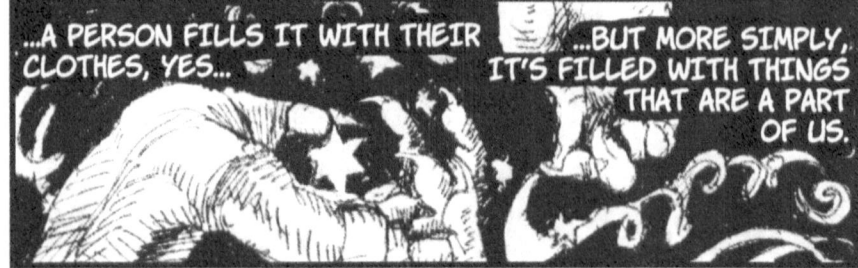

...A PERSON FILLS IT WITH THEIR CLOTHES, YES...

...BUT MORE SIMPLY, IT'S FILLED WITH THINGS THAT ARE A PART OF US.

40

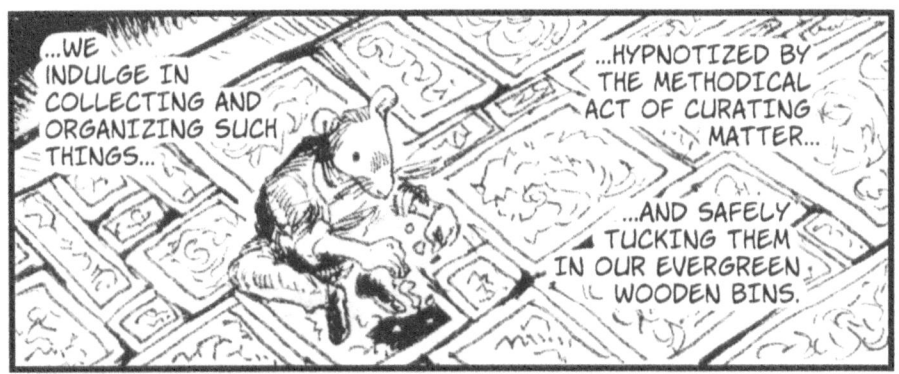

...WE INDULGE IN COLLECTING AND ORGANIZING SUCH THINGS...

...HYPNOTIZED BY THE METHODICAL ACT OF CURATING MATTER...

...AND SAFELY TUCKING THEM IN OUR EVERGREEN WOODEN BINS.

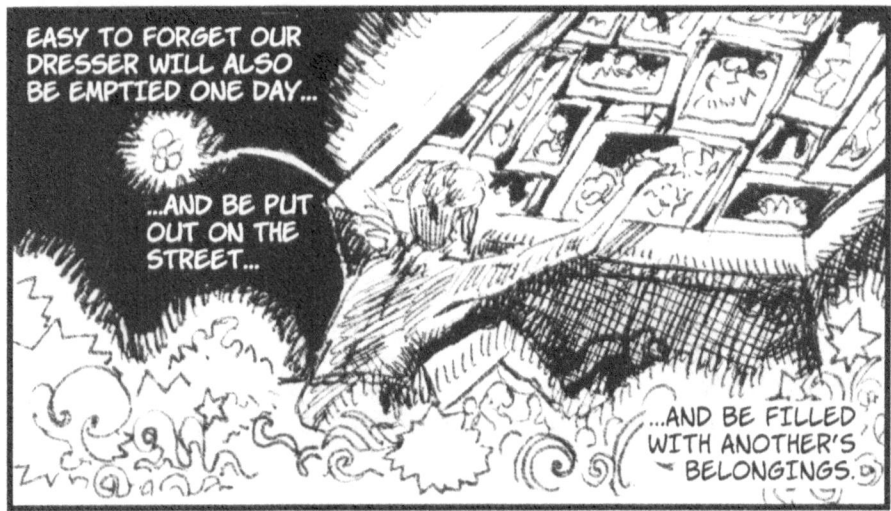

EASY TO FORGET OUR DRESSER WILL ALSO BE EMPTIED ONE DAY...

...AND BE PUT OUT ON THE STREET...

...AND BE FILLED WITH ANOTHER'S BELONGINGS.

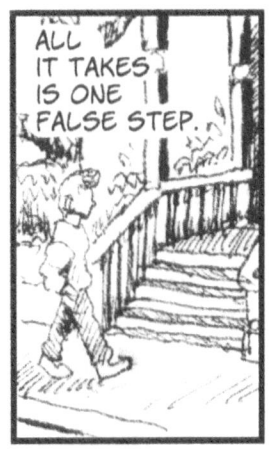

ALL IT TAKES IS ONE FALSE STEP.

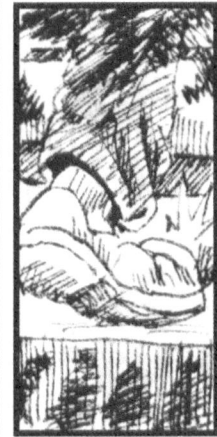

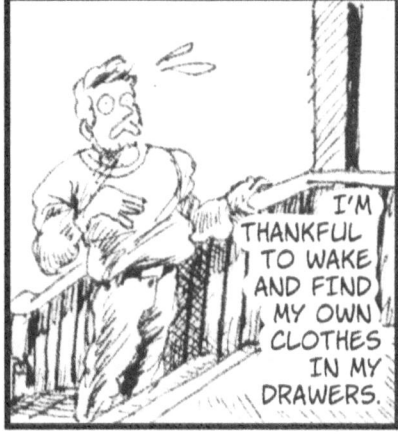

I'M THANKFUL TO WAKE AND FIND MY OWN CLOTHES IN MY DRAWERS.

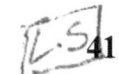

41

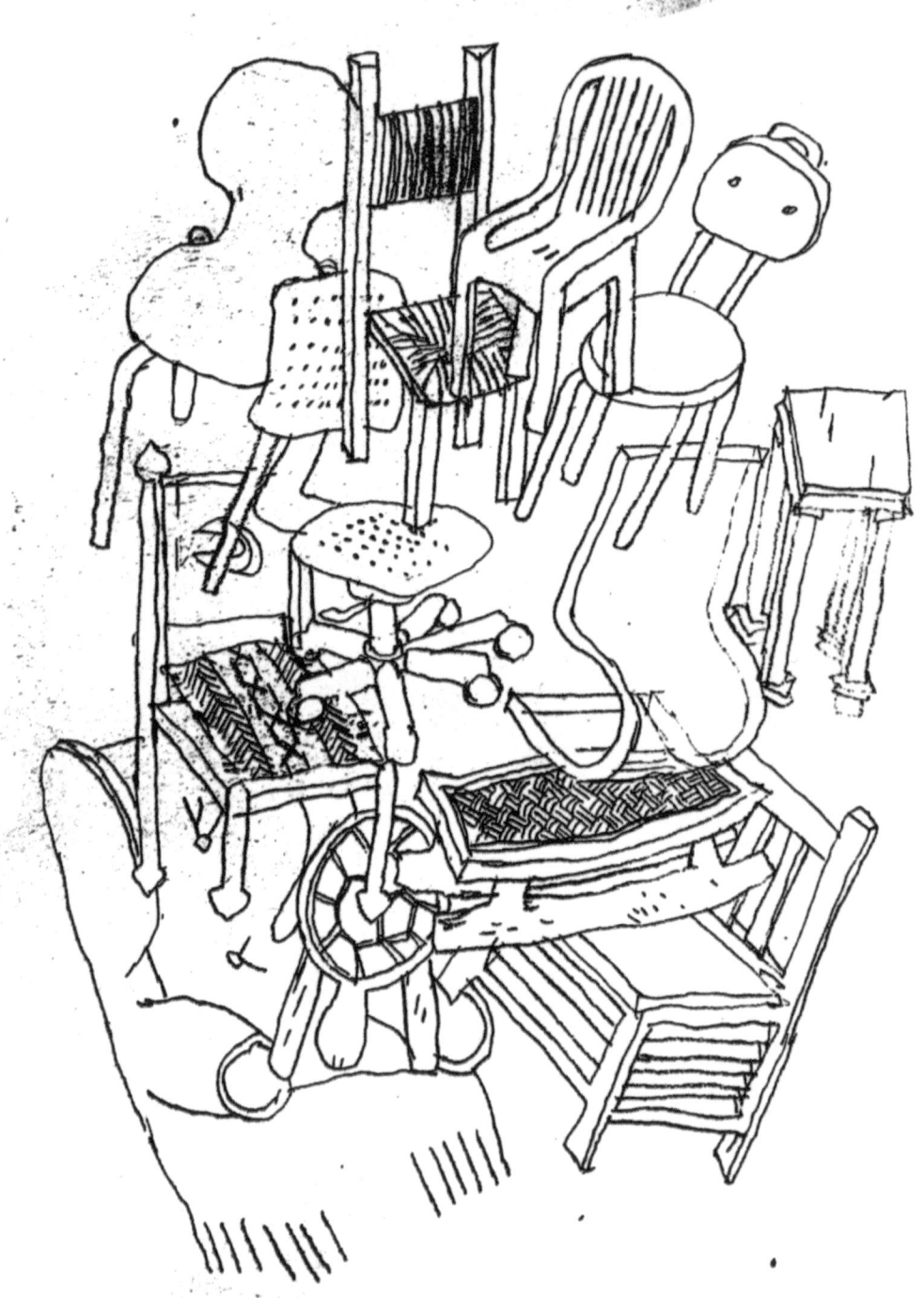

you asked why it seems
like my roommates hate you
you made it seem
like it was all my fault

and i really thought
we had similar trauma, same in nature
but hell i know now
red flags mean danger

please just know
you can come to me, if you really need
unfortunately
i will forgive you
you will manipulate me

i'm stuck on my couch again
listening to Punisher again
please don't associate Twin Fantasy with
someone
that shit will never work out

i met someone new
they're good to me
but I'm not sure i know what that means

i will hurt you
you will be mad at me

i really like you
hey stop looking at me

43

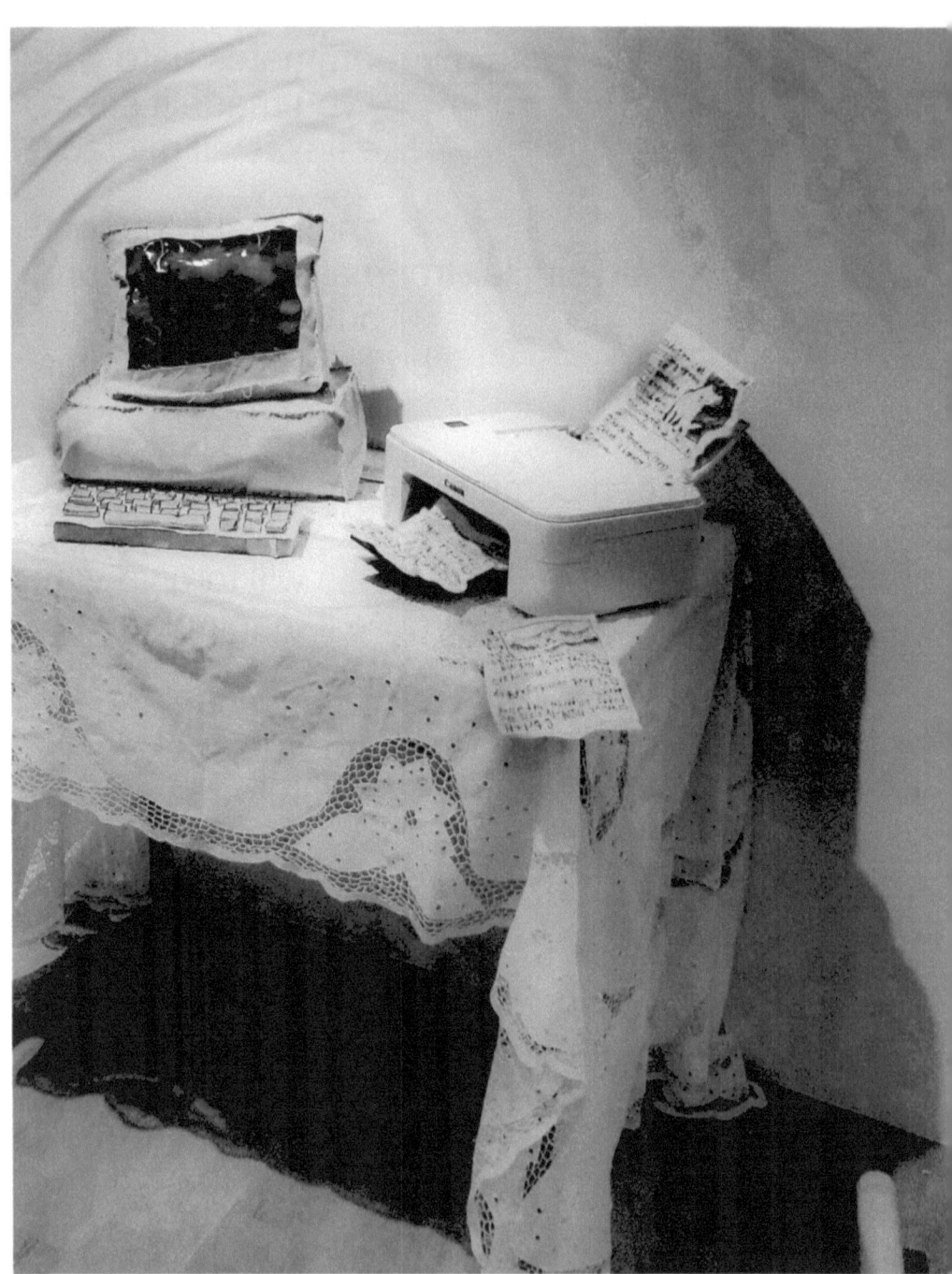

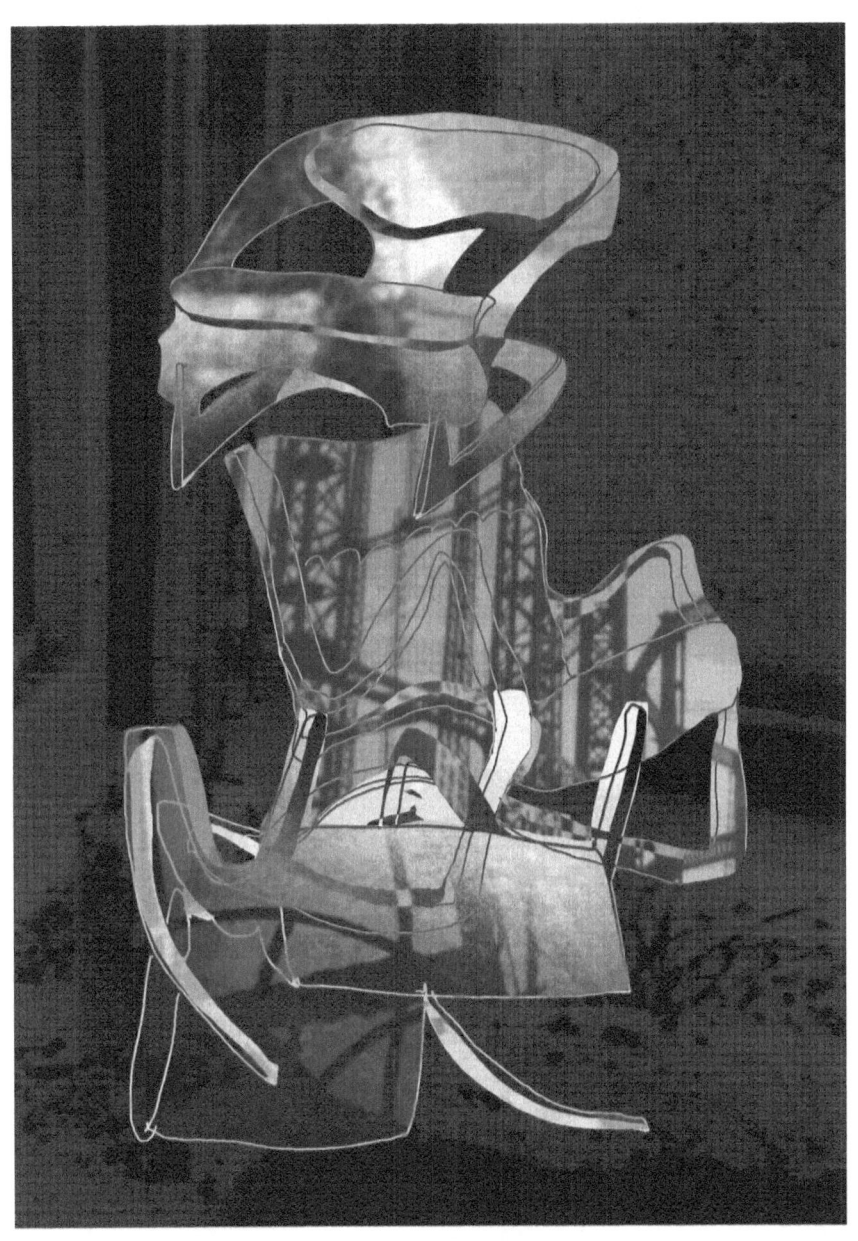

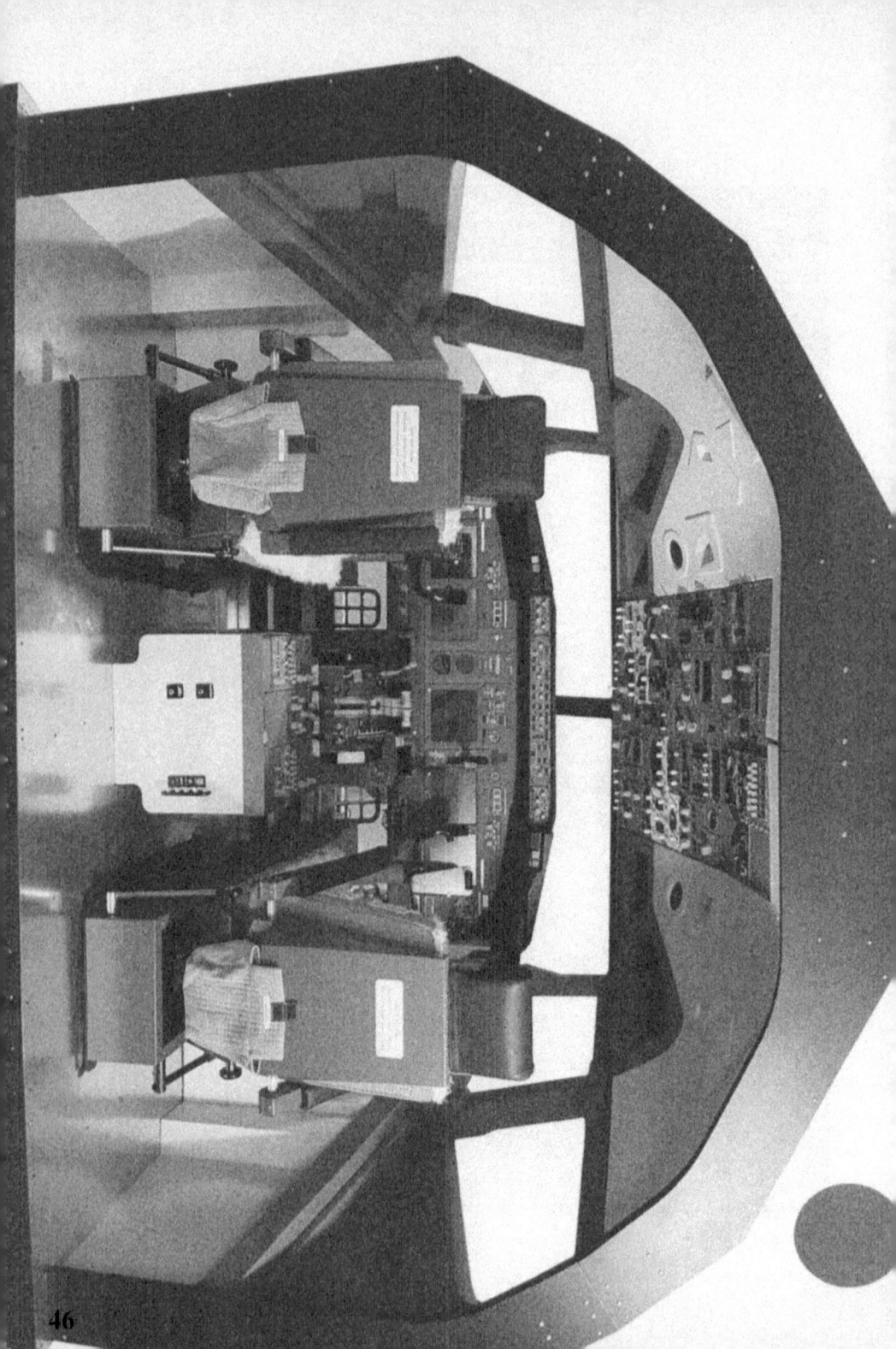

46

CHAPTER III: Utopia

DUNE

A pocket of sand
That I hold
Then spill out onto the floor
Windy dry mountain above lagoon
only allowed to exist in the shade of our dune
Don't step on small grasses
they hold this all in place
Little leaves and little flowers with little butterflies wrapped
inside
Hide from sands sweeping our ankles
Feel how the grains cut in
The rough edges are getting buffed off
If you run down wind pushes you
in just the right way
Feel fifty pounds lighter
Beetles here and there and pause when a gust hits
See fossils, petrified wood, ancient shells dotting the
static,

But most to never be seen.

Falling stars above you, tumbling
Dark grass beneath you, ristling
Strong gusts of wind around you, wuthering
My burning heart beside you, rumbling.

You are a dream I cannot fathom
You are the blessing and the god I thank
The sun itself, shining brightly
I worship you, trembling slightly.

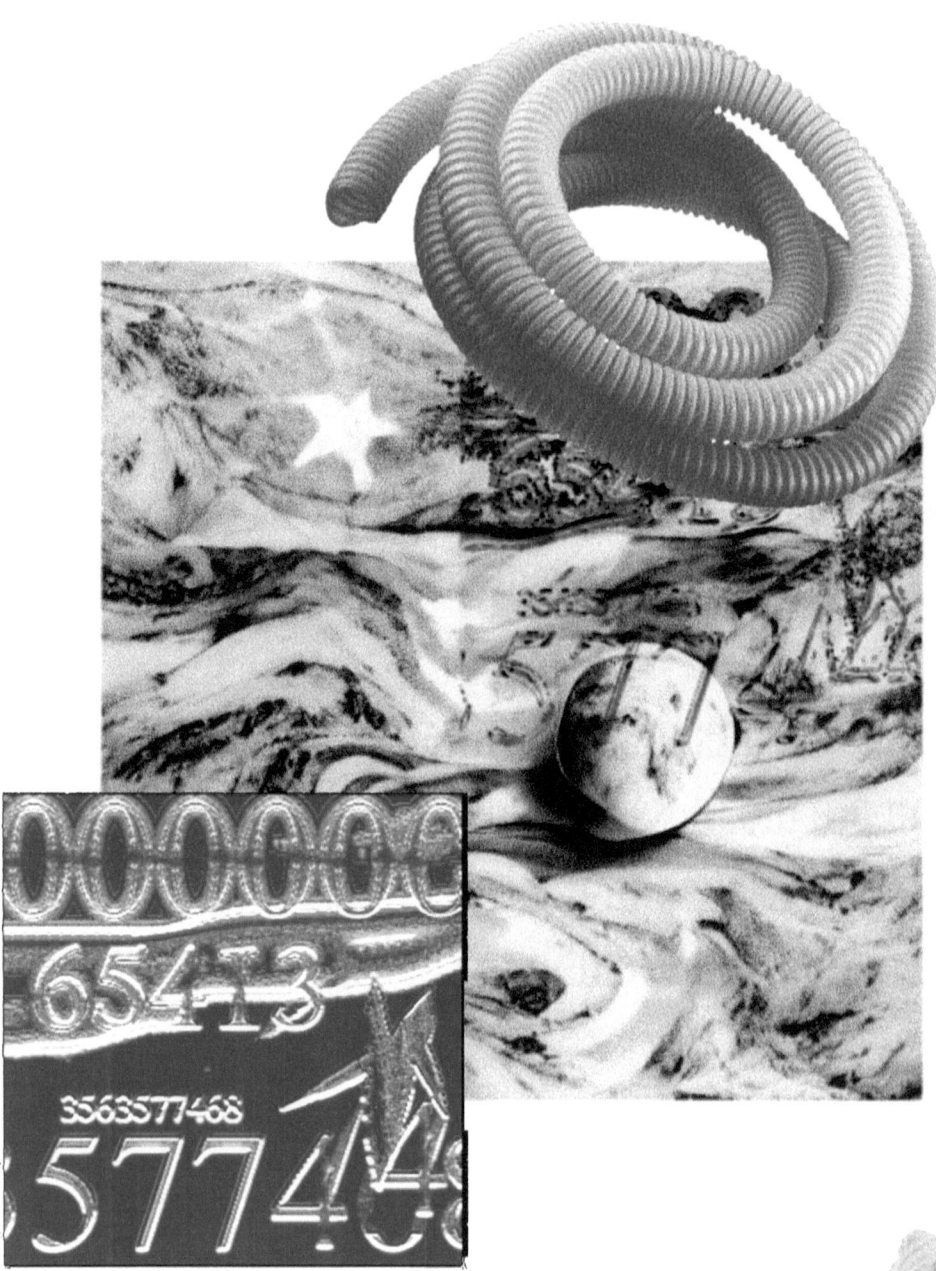

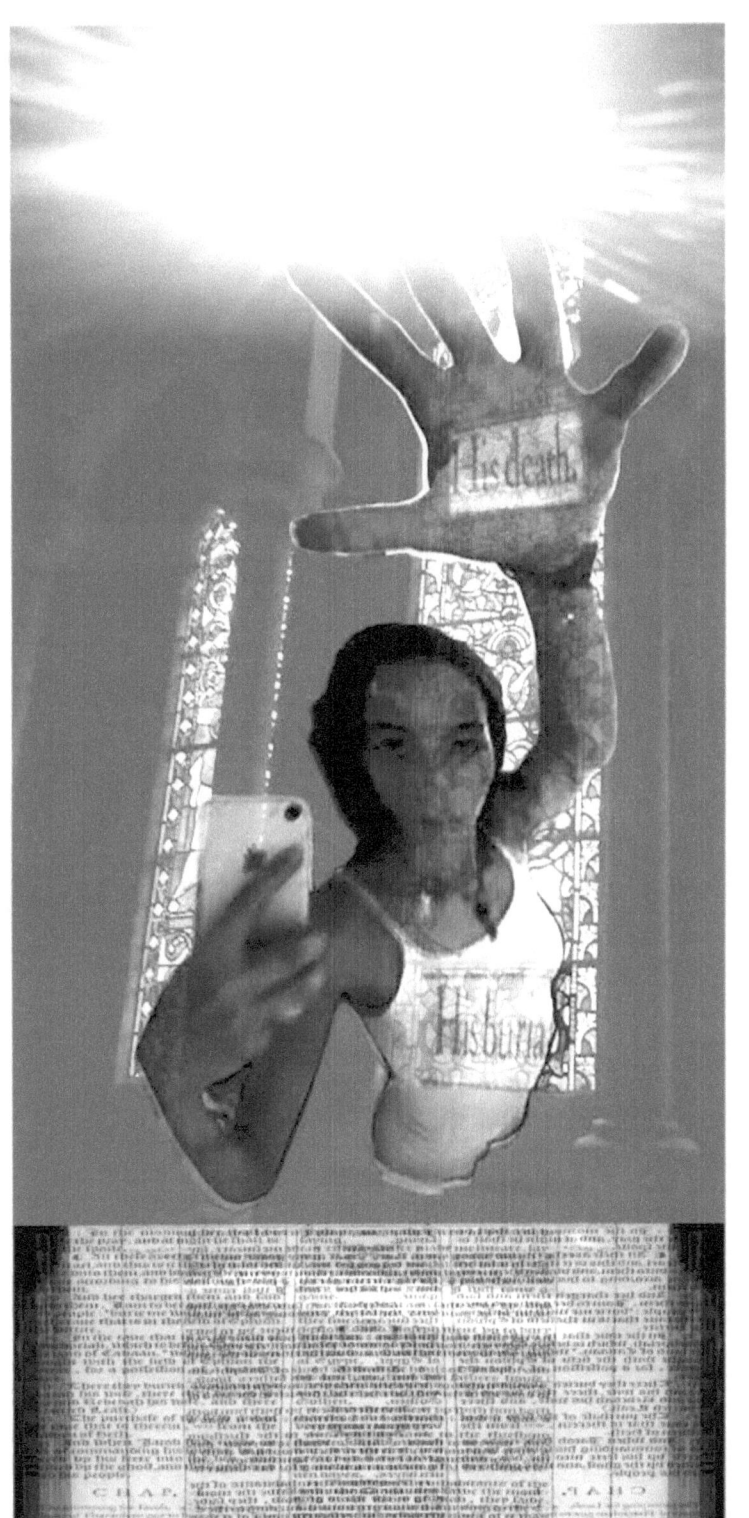

51

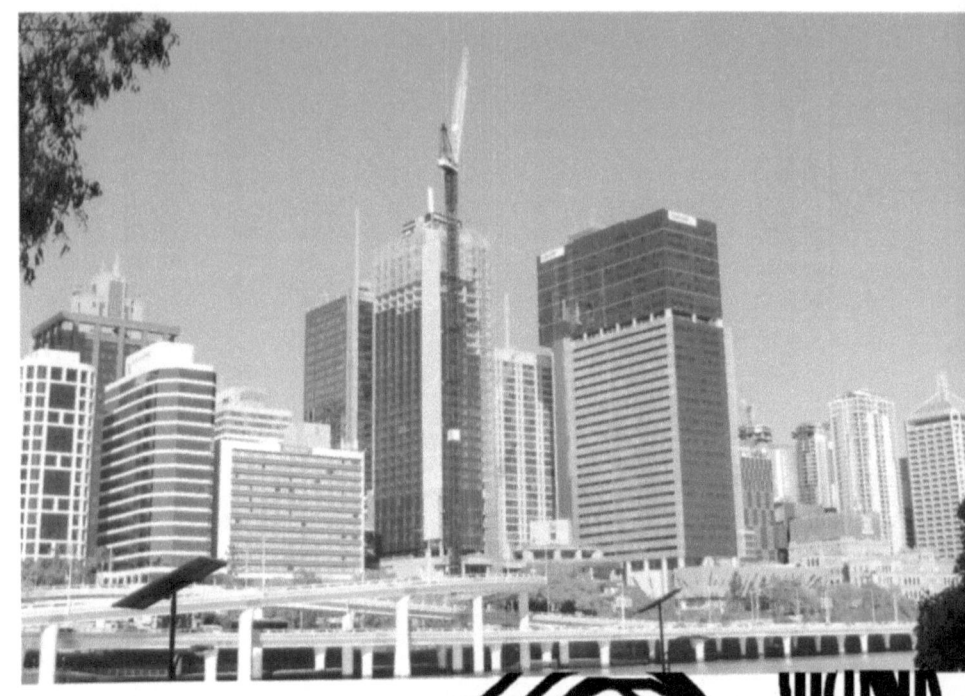

Don't preempt it, sit with it and enjoy good things happening to you as much as you dread bad things happening to you.

Tall, lone city, subtropical climate. Lots of complex, tonal, and greys for light and shadow, rendered in a semi-impressionistic style, emphasising how tall and dense the buildings are when viewed from a lower perspective. The buildings, reaching clouds in a crisp, self-assured, blue sky, with a warm and clinical feeling. Buildings general structures have orange accents and maybe some red-hued blue accents too, certain including some dark green elements with palm trees. Have waste disposal near the camera, more like a large pit than a dumpster. Add a gritty element without being gritty enough to suggest the world neglects cleanliness in any way - it is more so showing a symptom of the city having lost the point of being really 'lived-in' - although people are oddly nowhere to be seen.
In this world it's let go or be dragged and sometimes there is no way to reach an impasse.

naples yellow & unbleached titanium, lilac, titanium white, cerulean blue & manganese blue hue, cadmium orange & spectrum vermillion, phthalo blue (red shade) & permanent mauve, phthalo green & spectrum green

We return to our regularly scheduled programming:

Inspiring trust in you of tomorrow

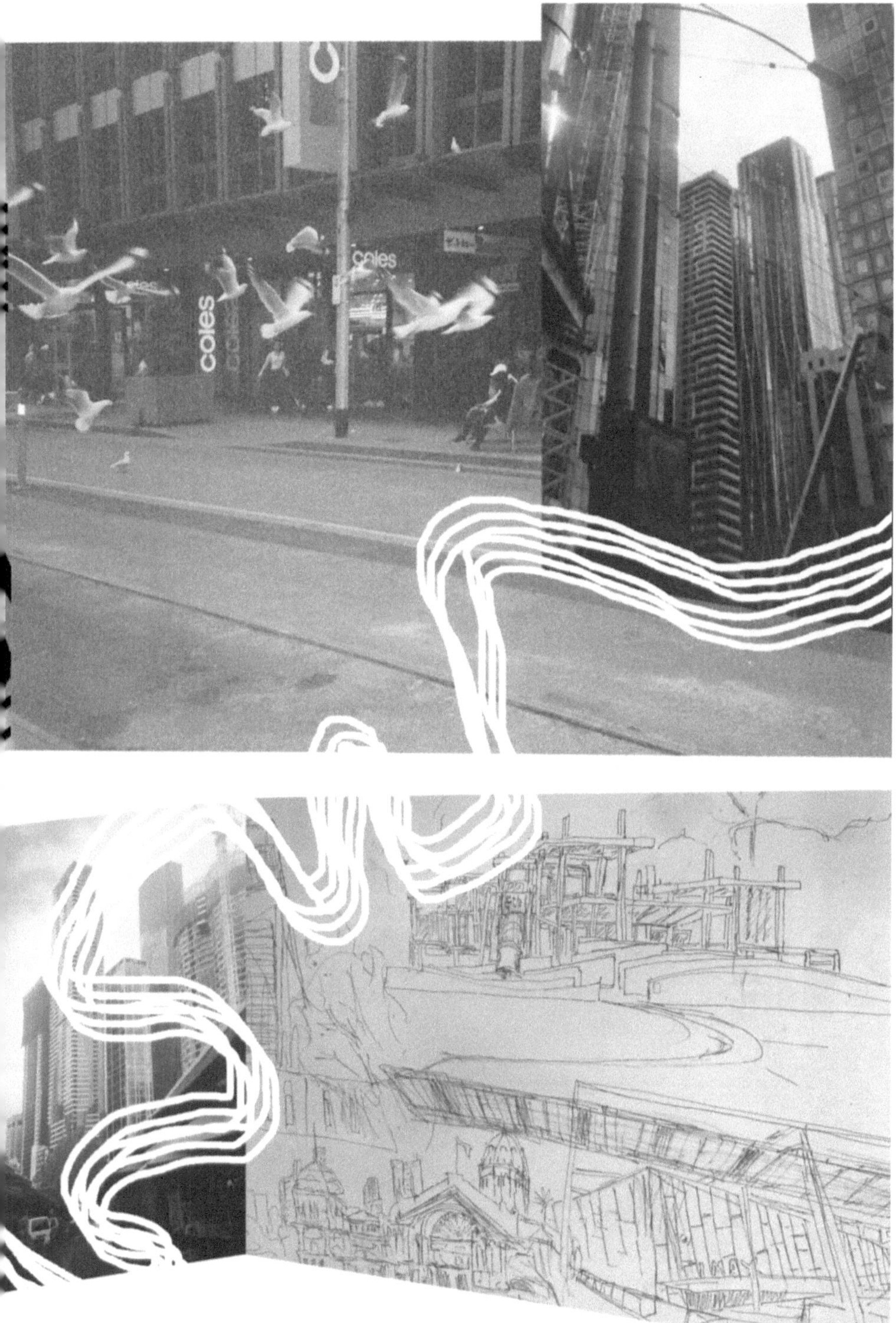
coles
coles
coles

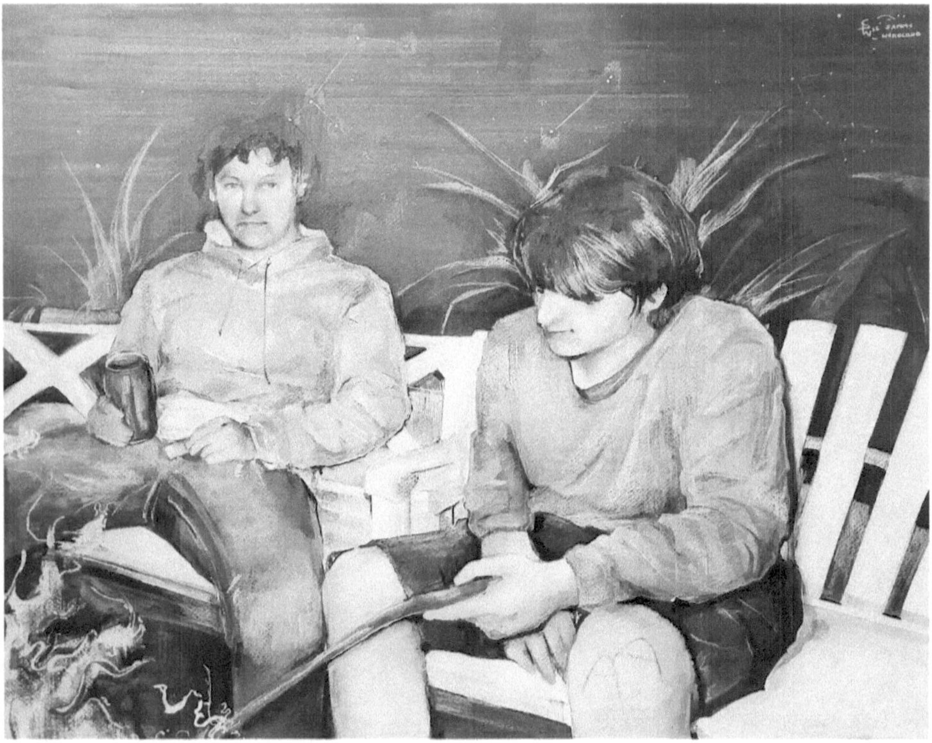

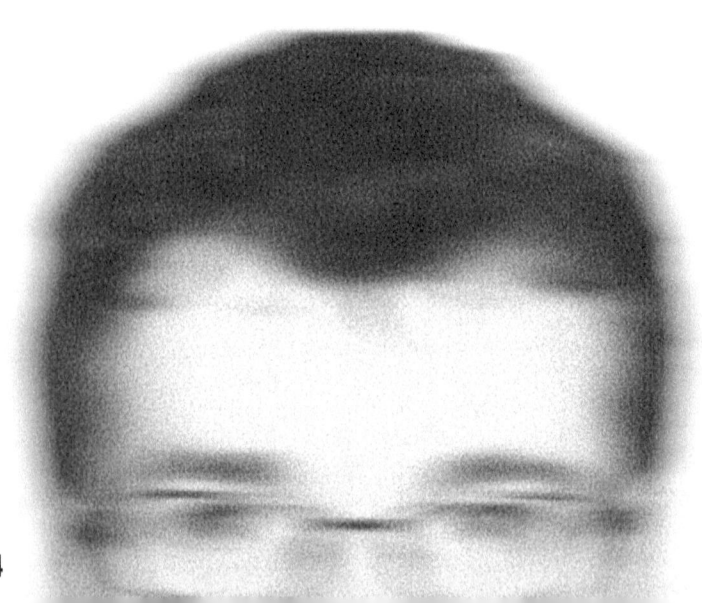

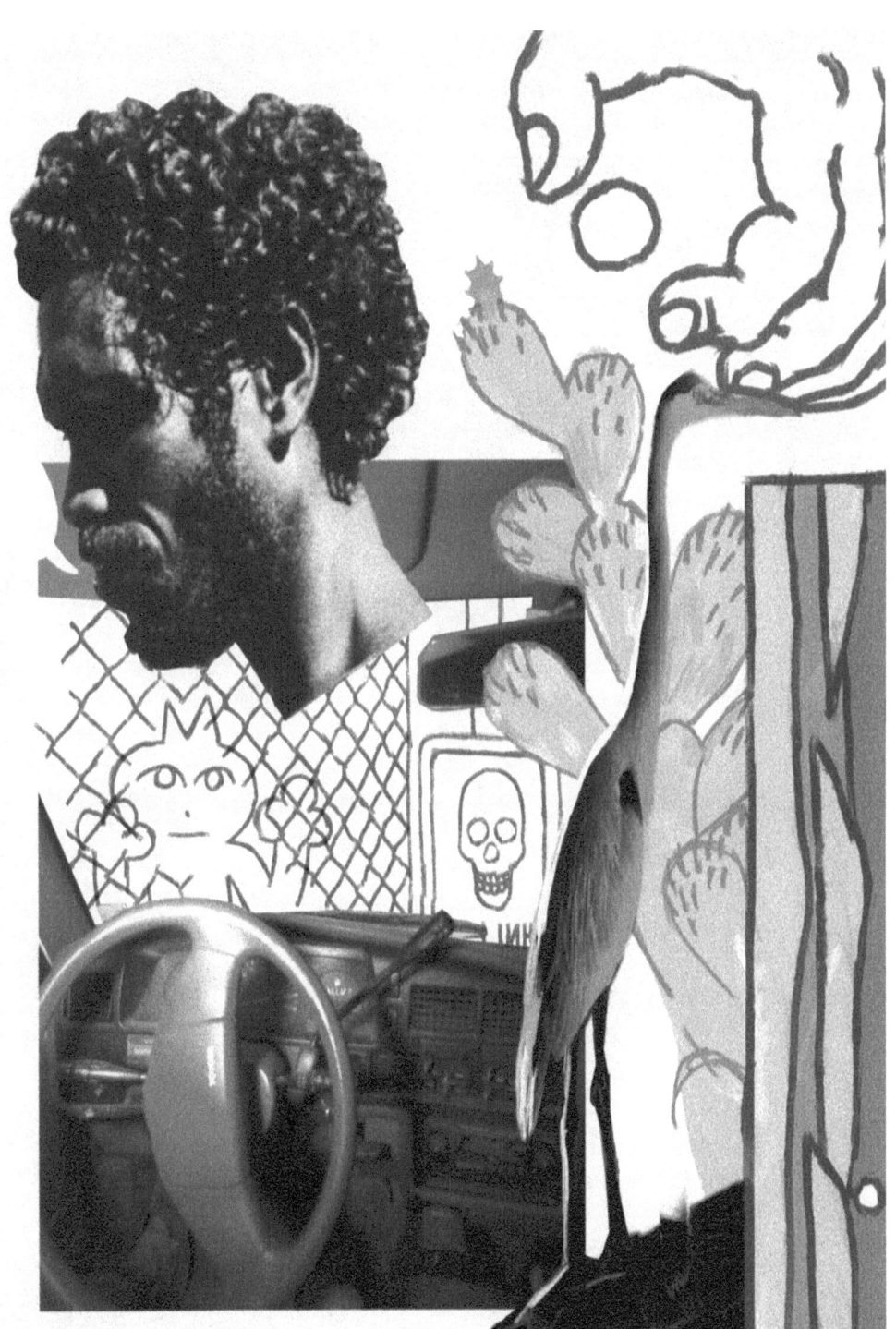

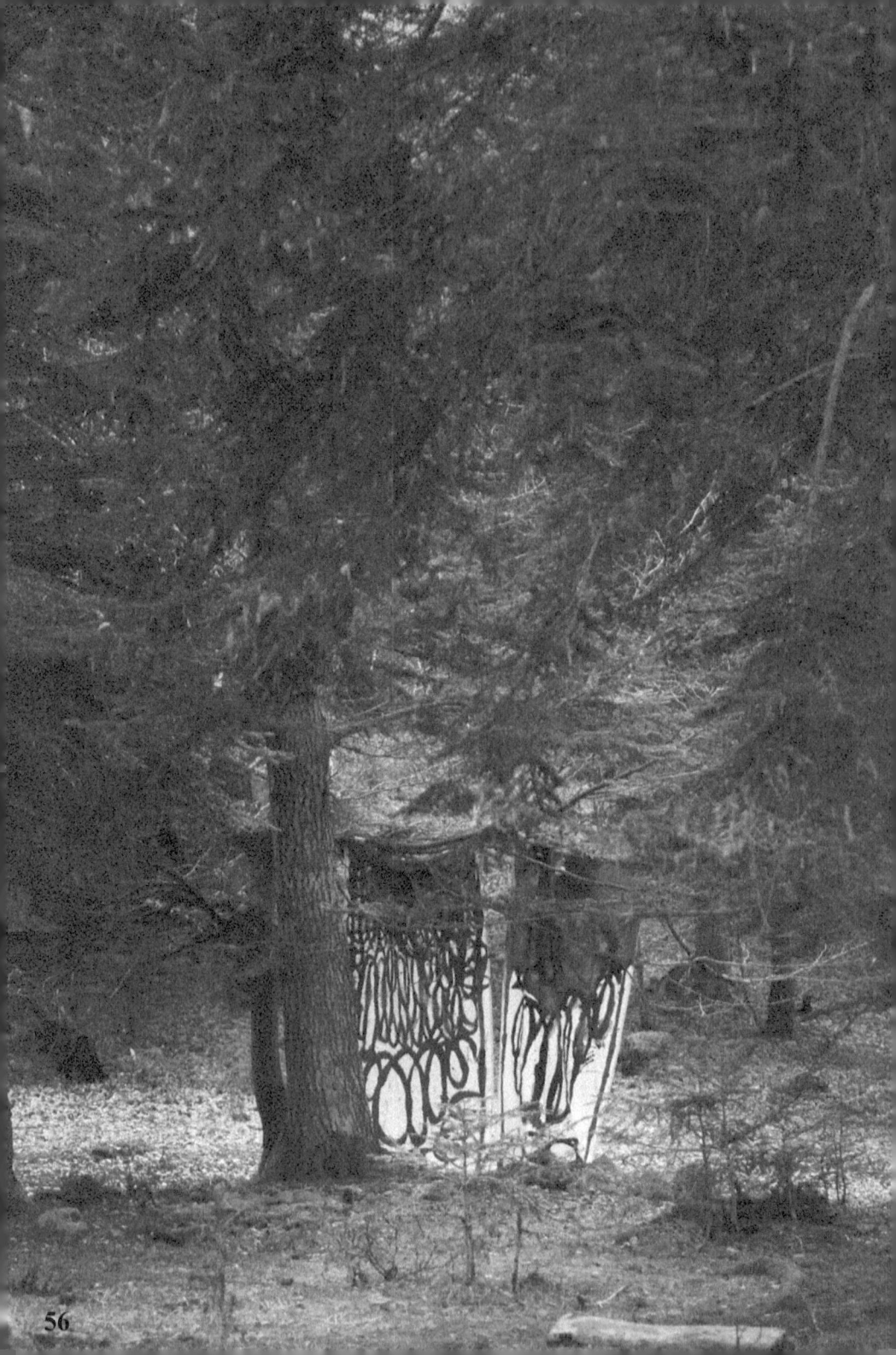

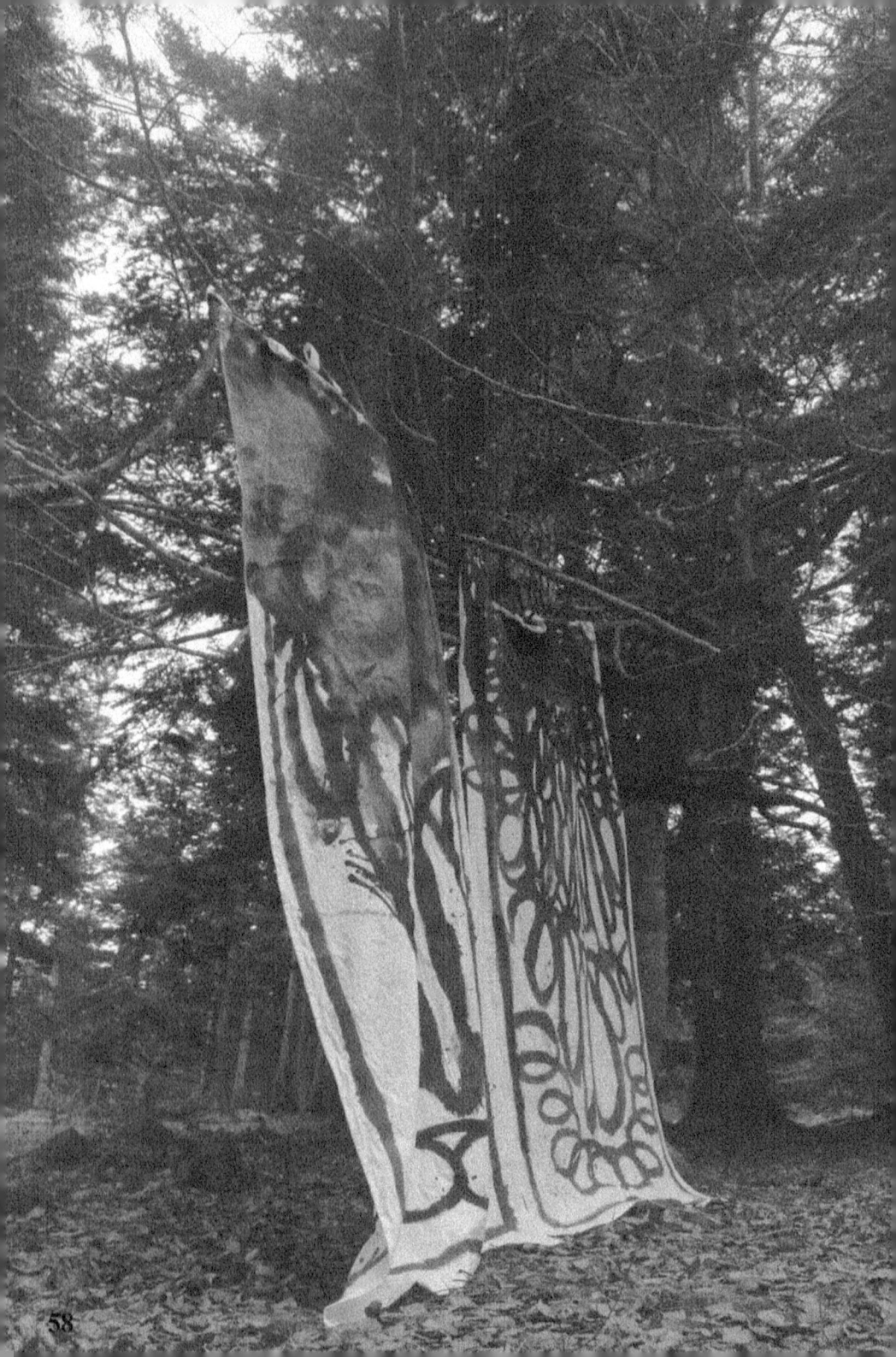

Una presión,
un dolor,
un fuego,
un vacío,
un suspiro,
dos vacíos,
una mirada de reojo,
una memoria fugaz,
o tres,
o cuatro,
unas lágrimas,
unos sentimientos,
dos dias
o tres años,
ninguna respuesta,
una propuesta,
muchas preguntas,
ninguna respuesta,
ninguna respuesta.

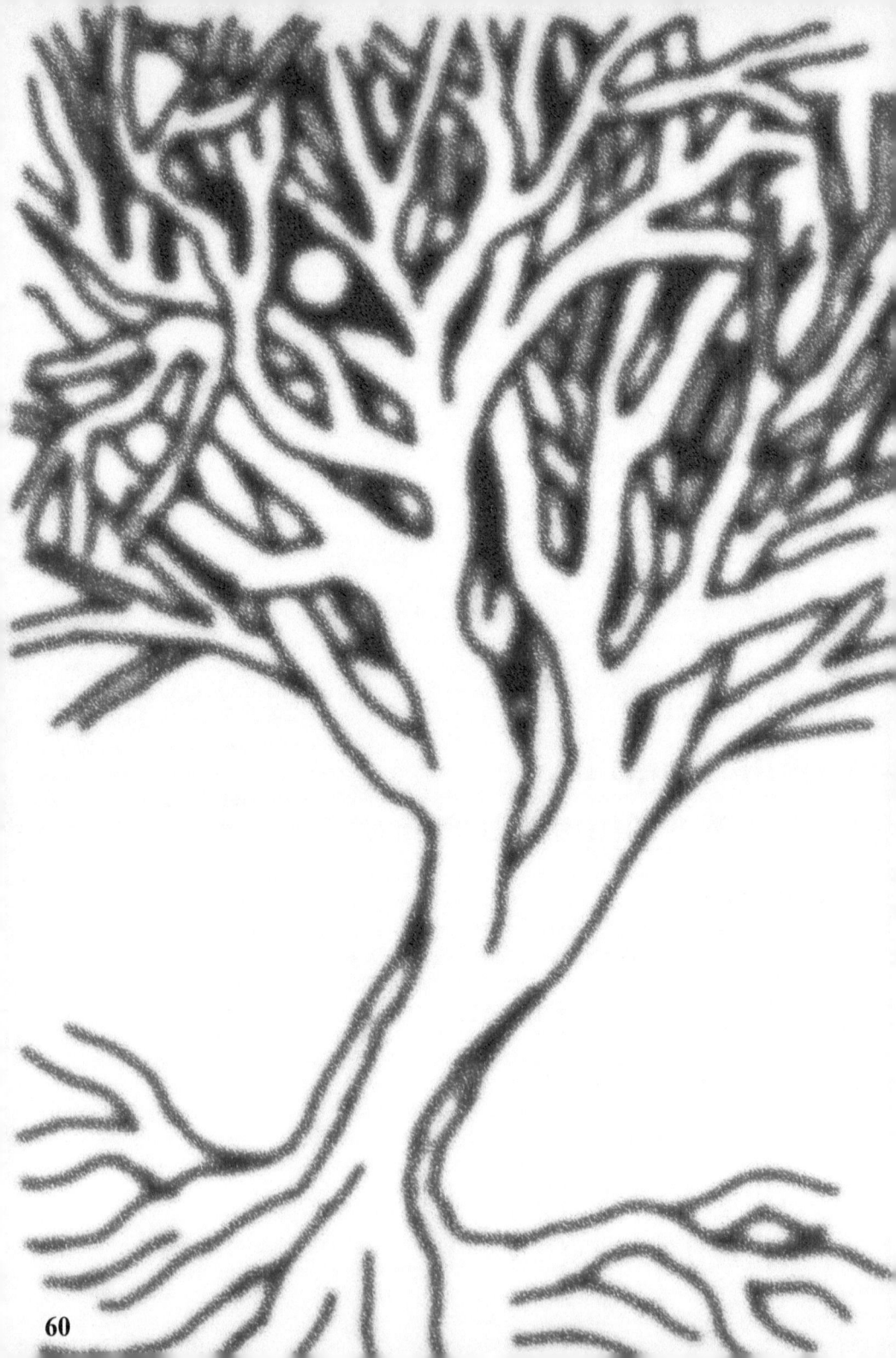

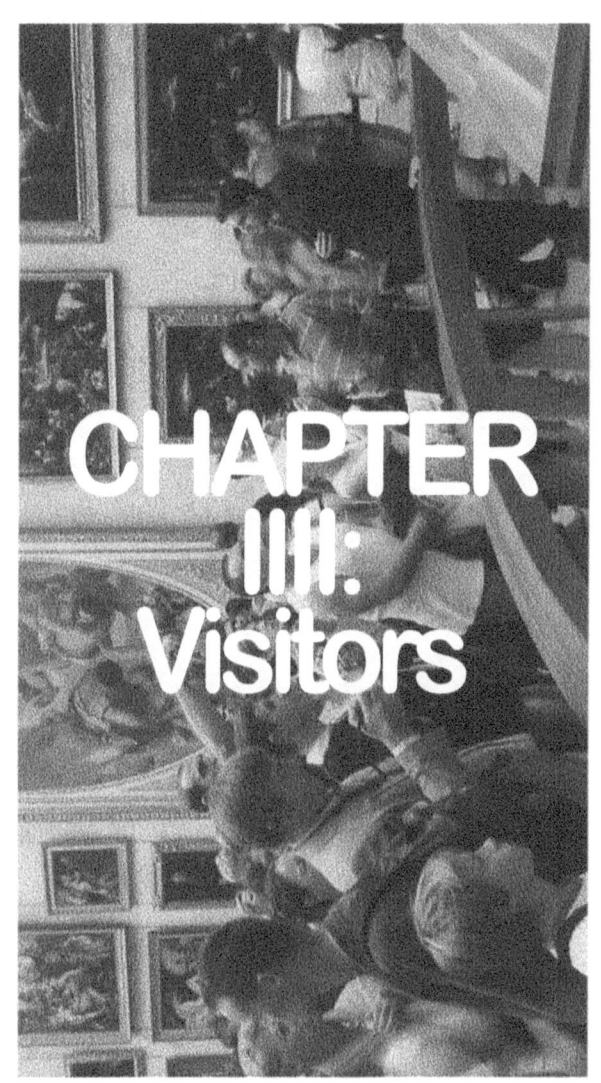

CHAPTER IIII: Visitors

NOT ALL WHO WANDER ARE LOST ✳

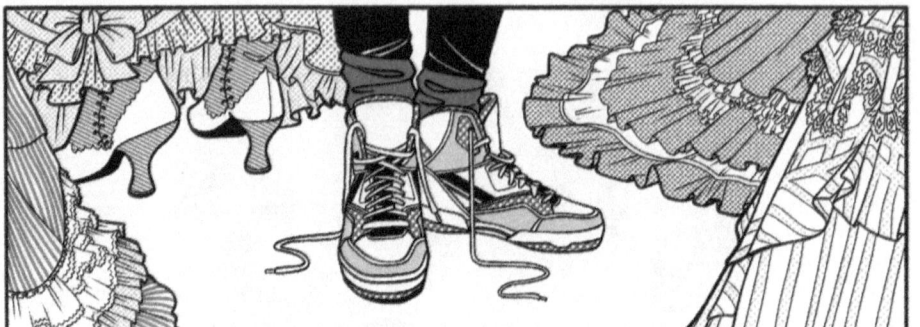

Off-track   **Time Travellers**

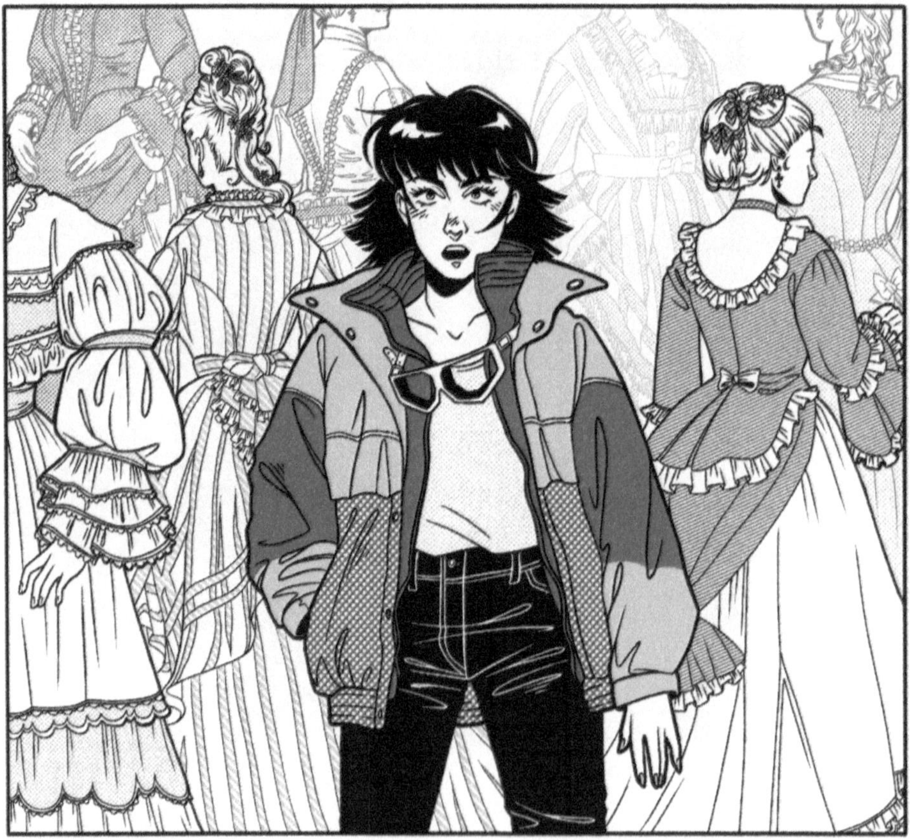

✦ ✦ ✦   BUT I SURE AM

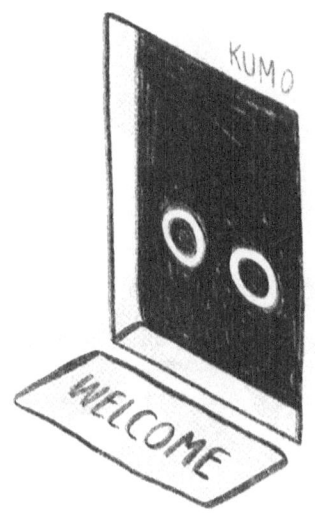

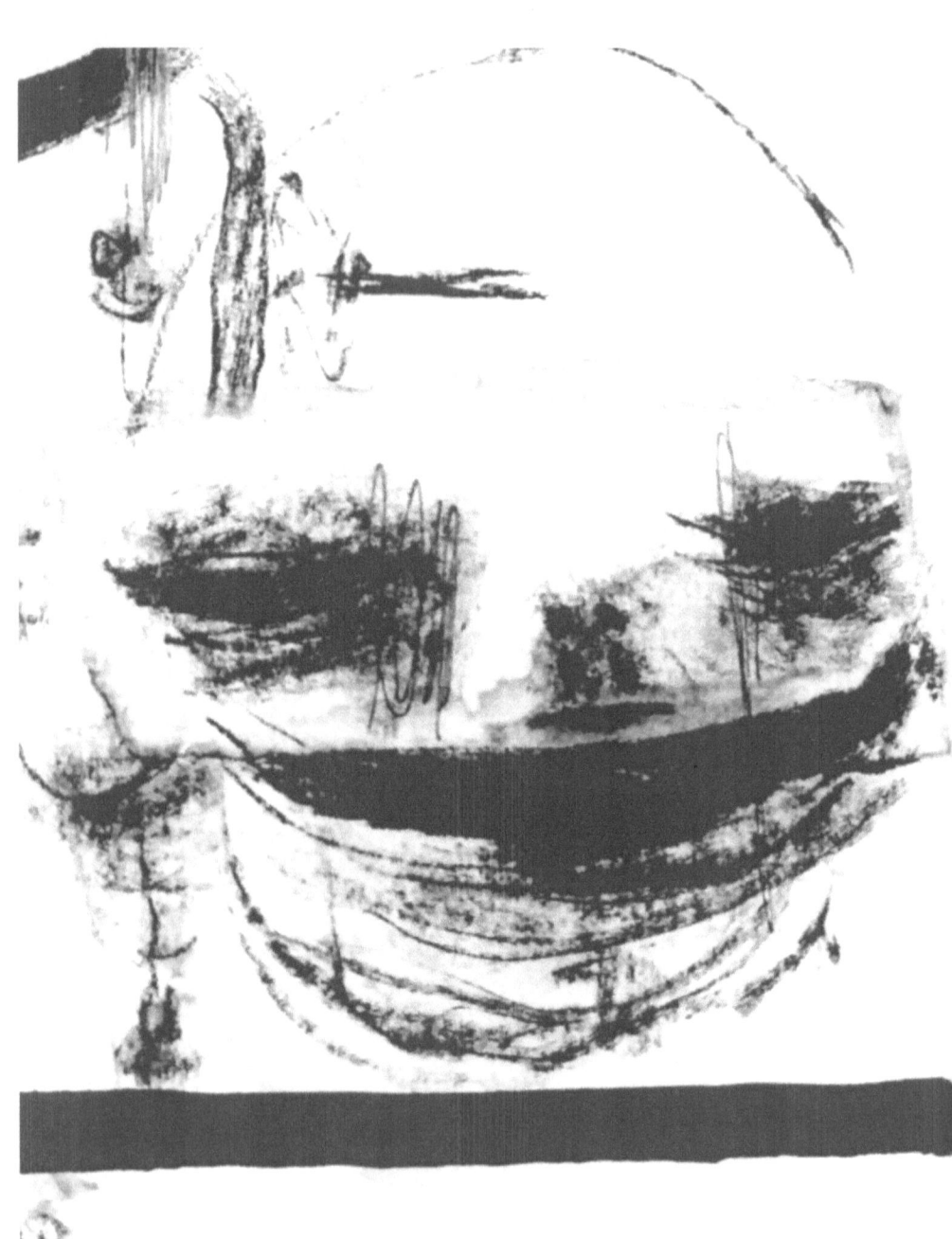

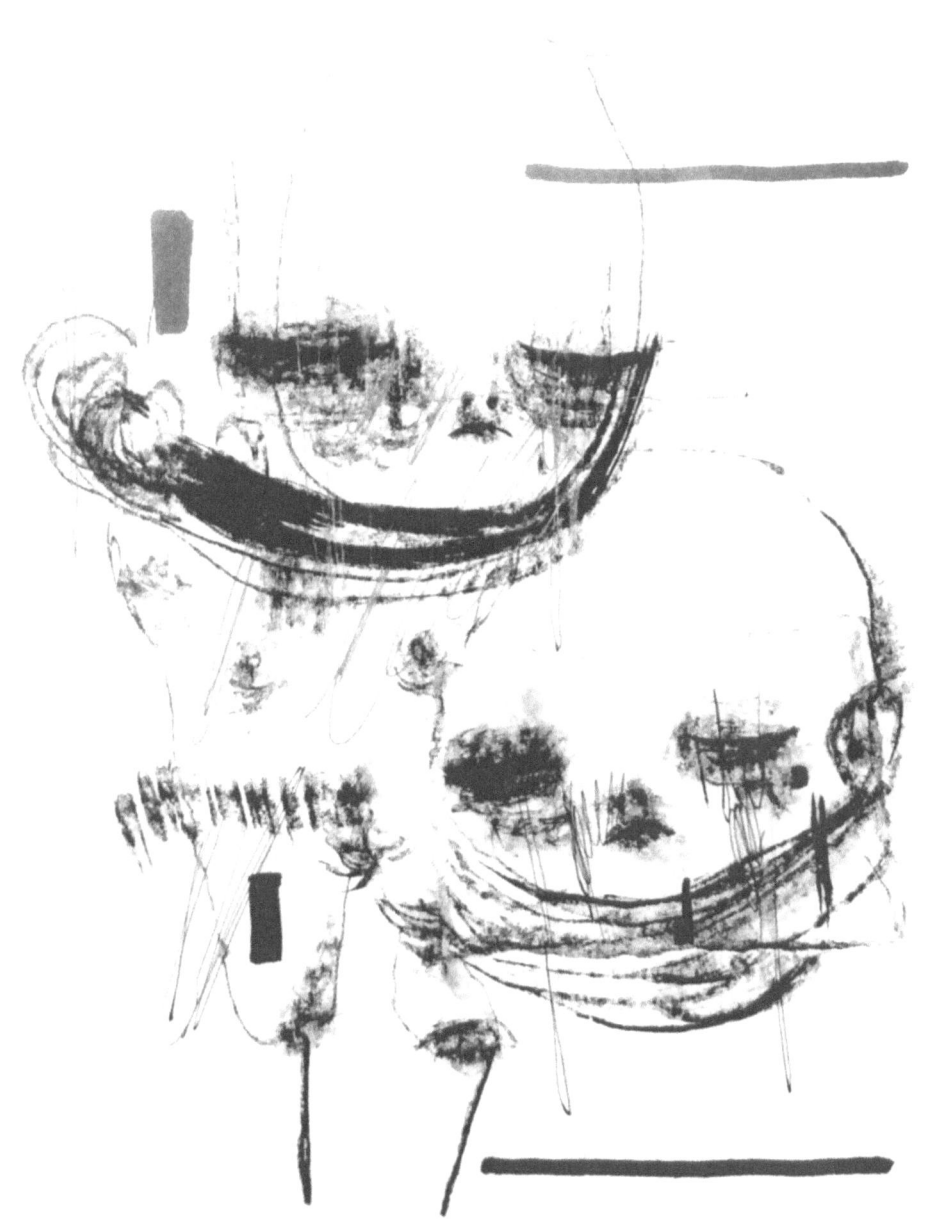

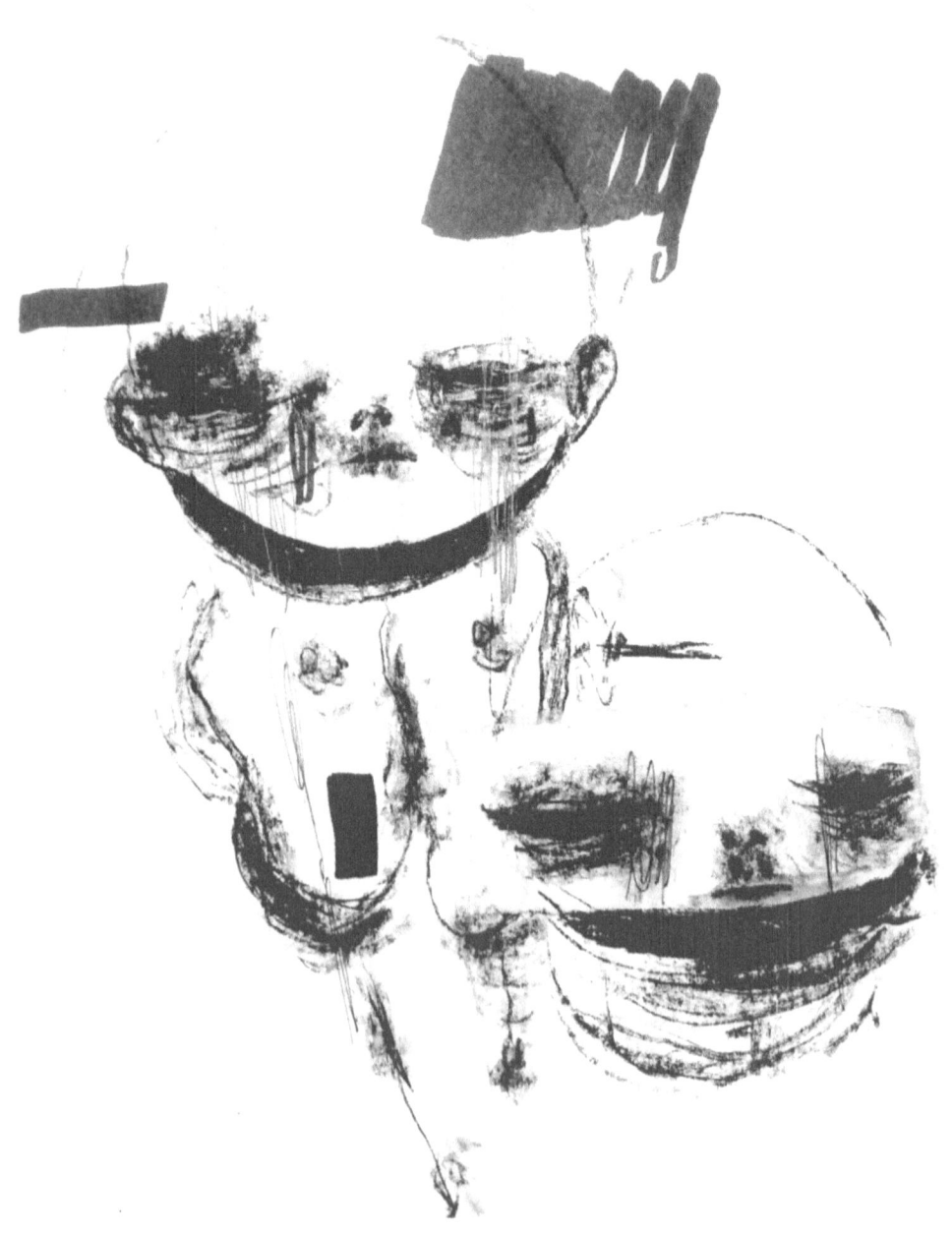

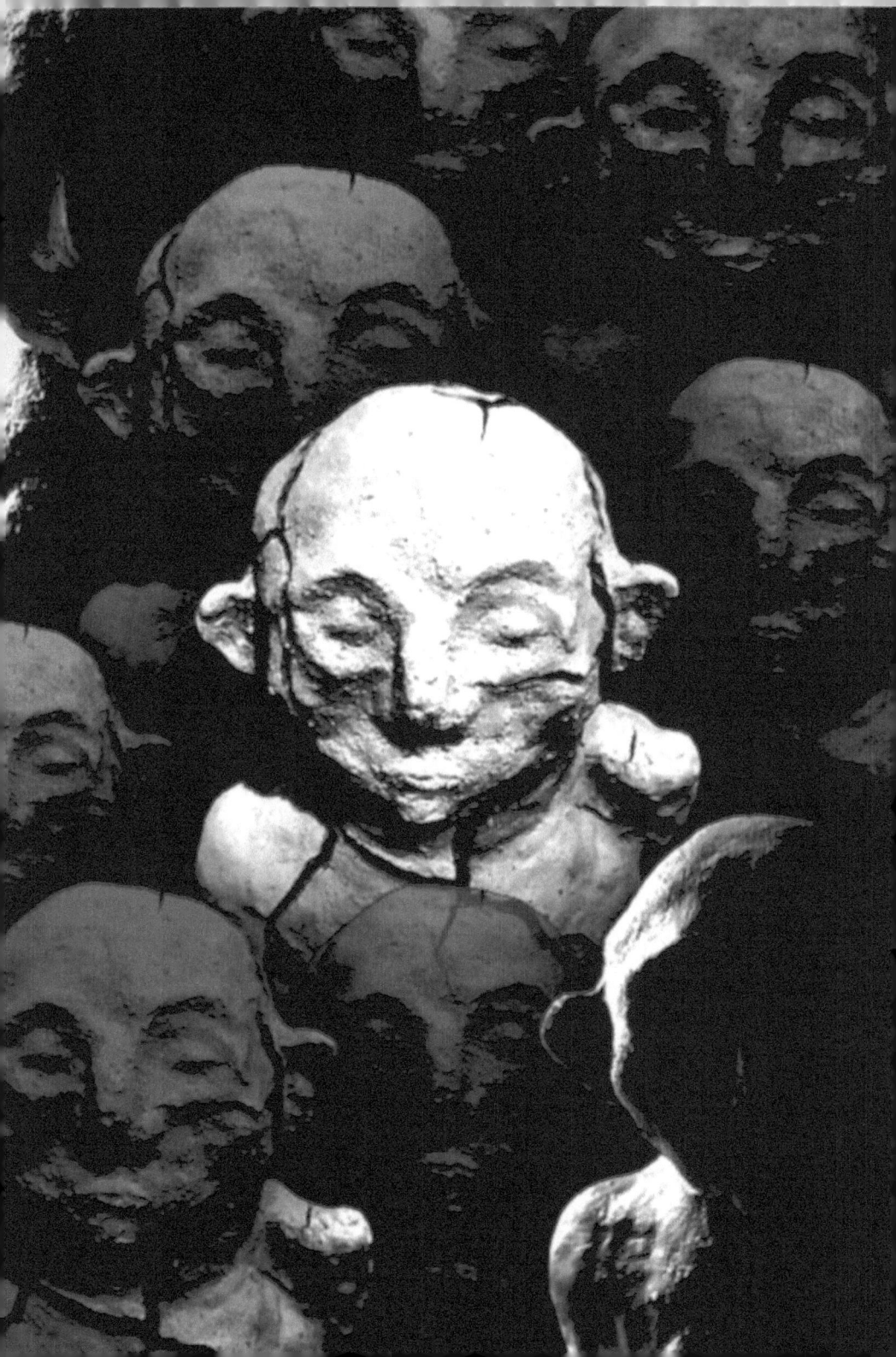

TO PROTECT THE STAR CHILD

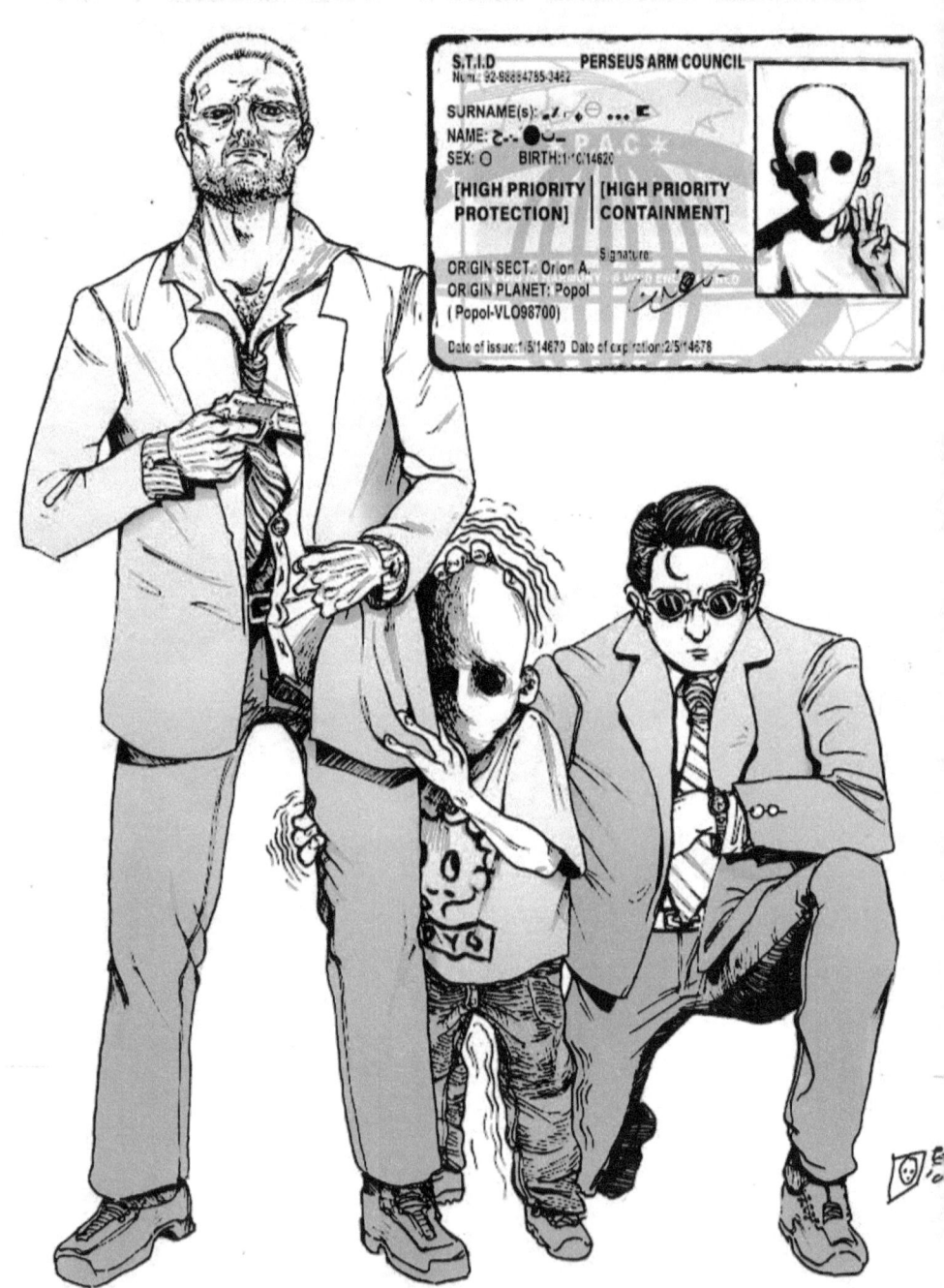

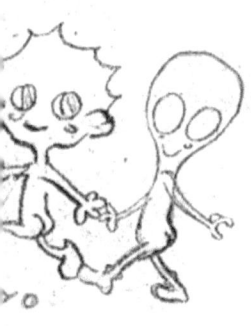

PERSEUS ARM COUNCIL
A VOID IN HARMONY   A VOID ENLIGHTENED

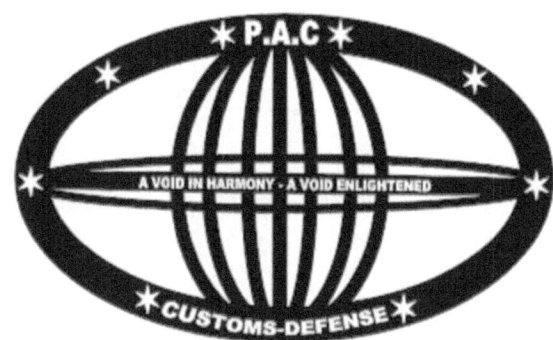

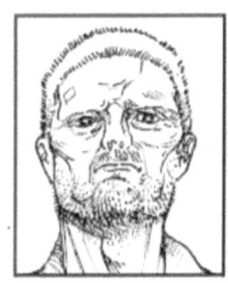

SURNAME: ▓▓▓▓ ▓▓▓▓
NAME: ▓▓
CODENAME "CHANK"

RECORD:

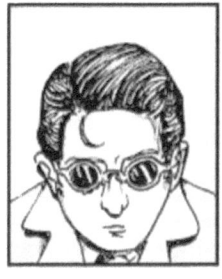

SURNAME: ▓▓▓▓ ▓▓▓▓
NAME: ▓▓▓▓
CODENAME "ROACH"

RECORD:

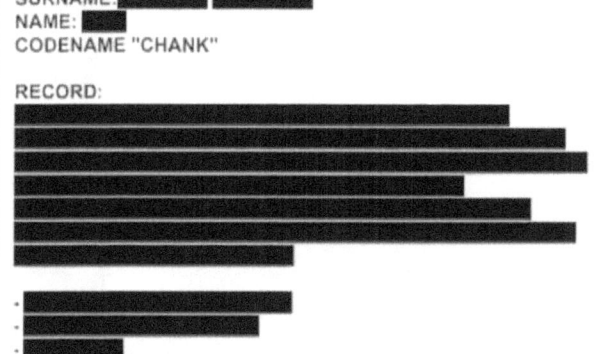

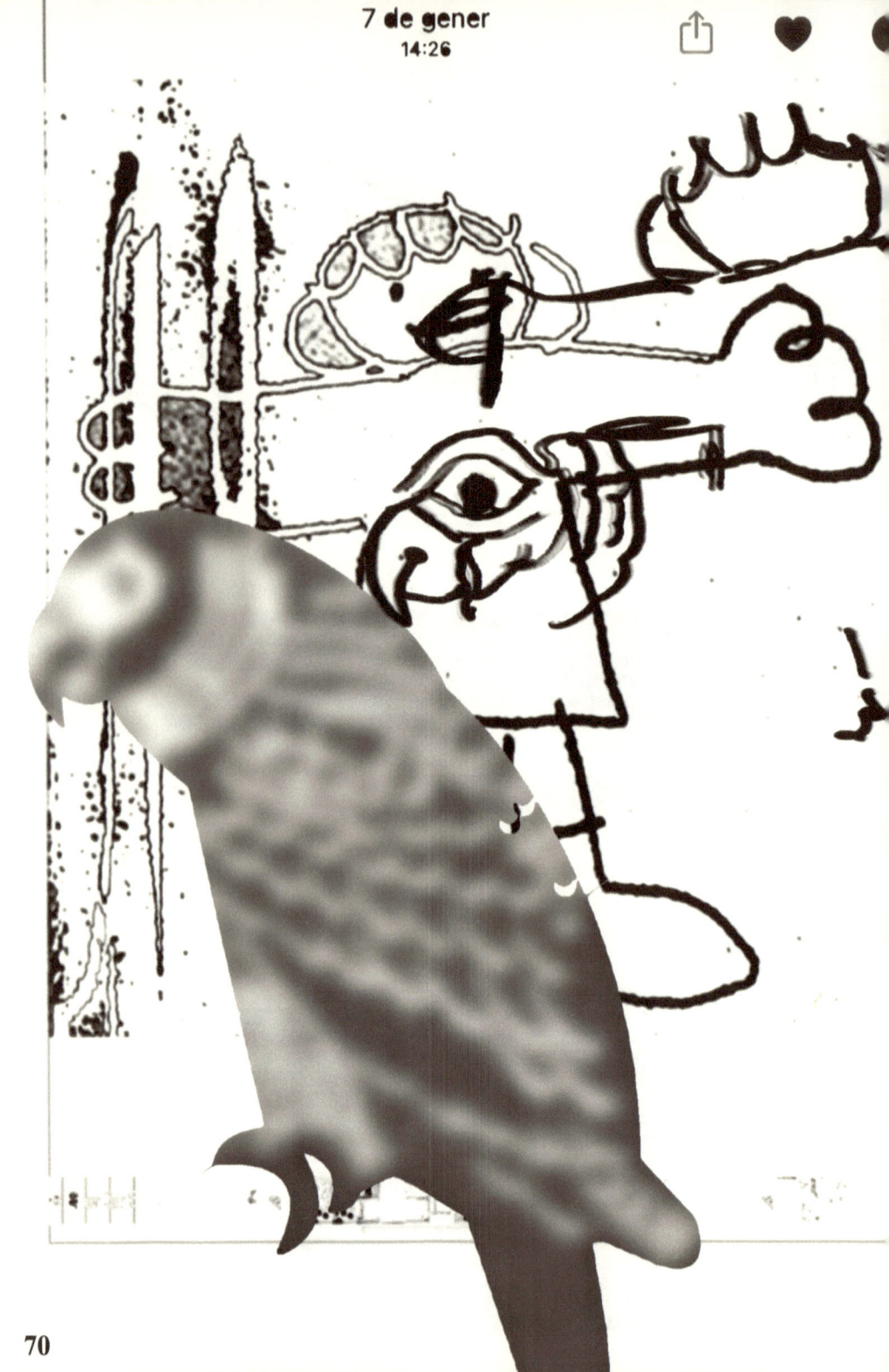

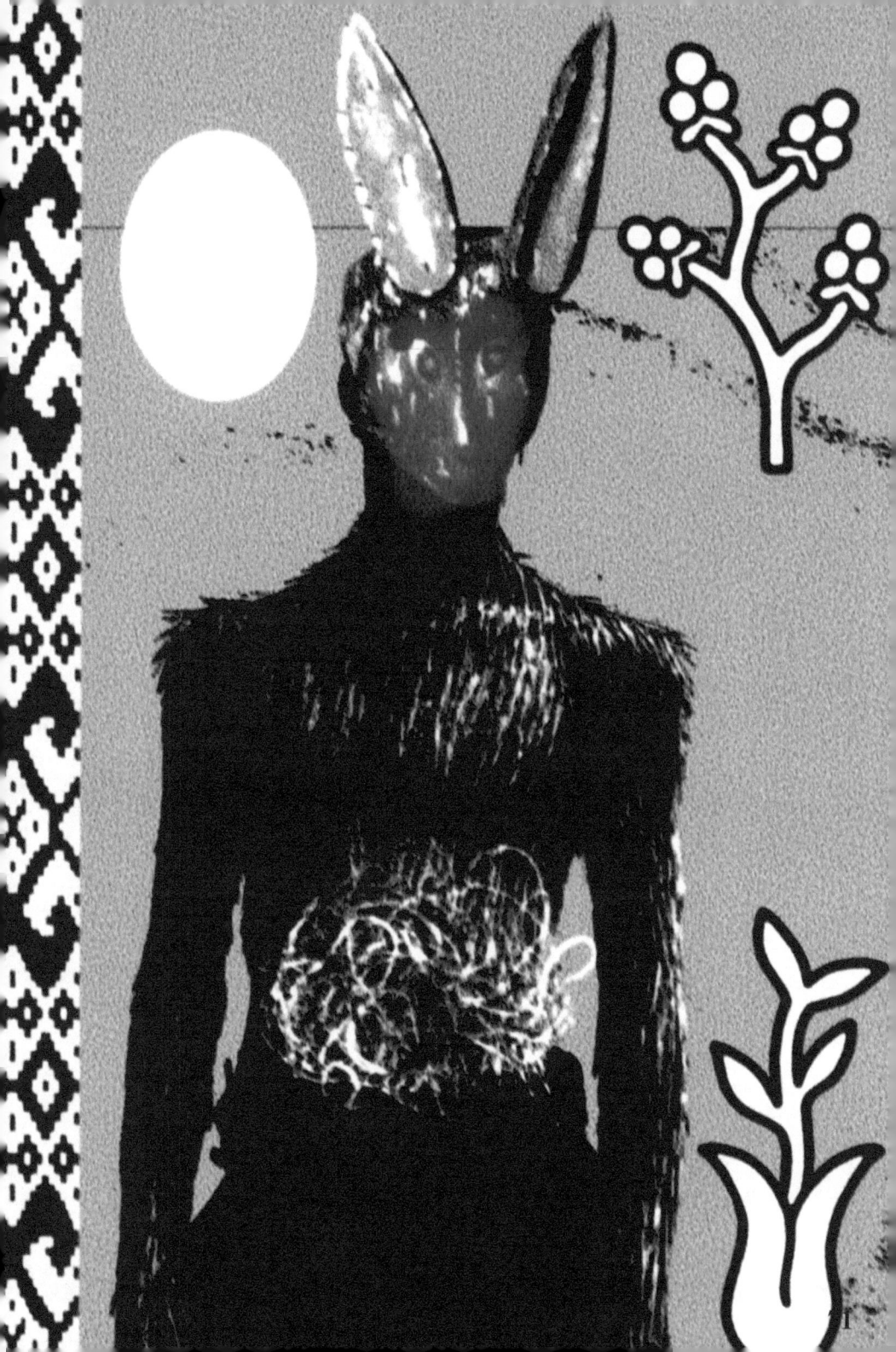

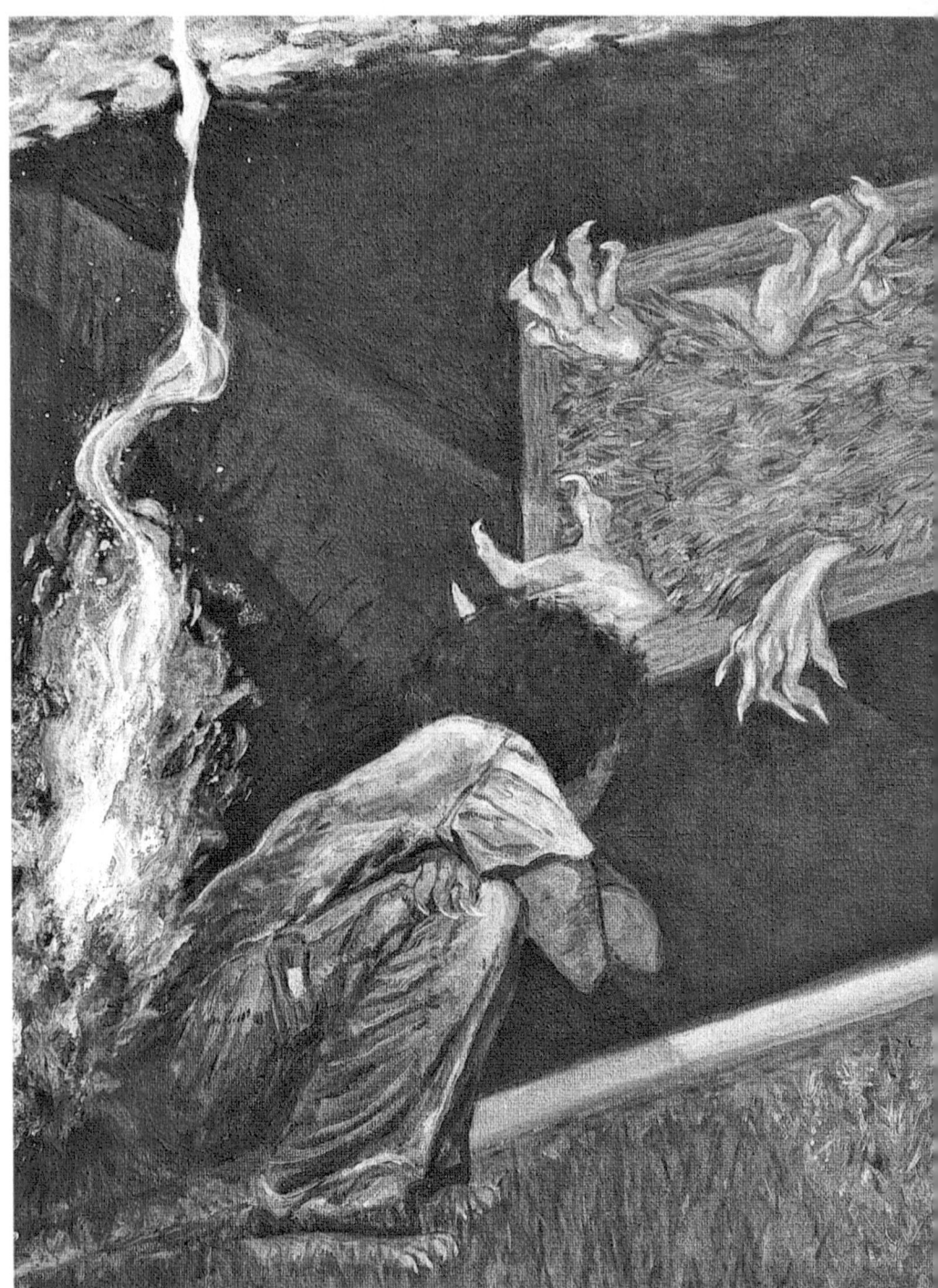

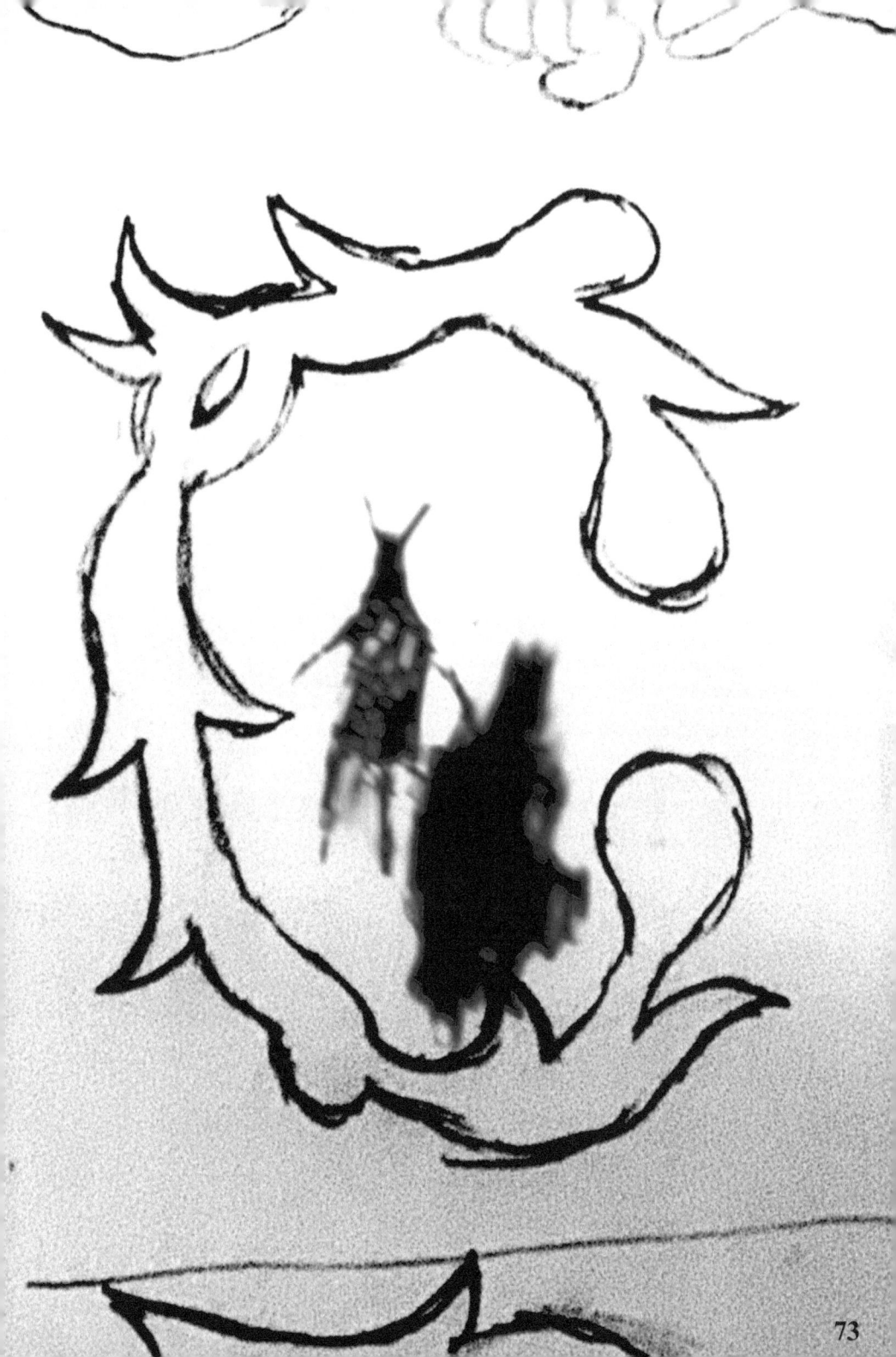

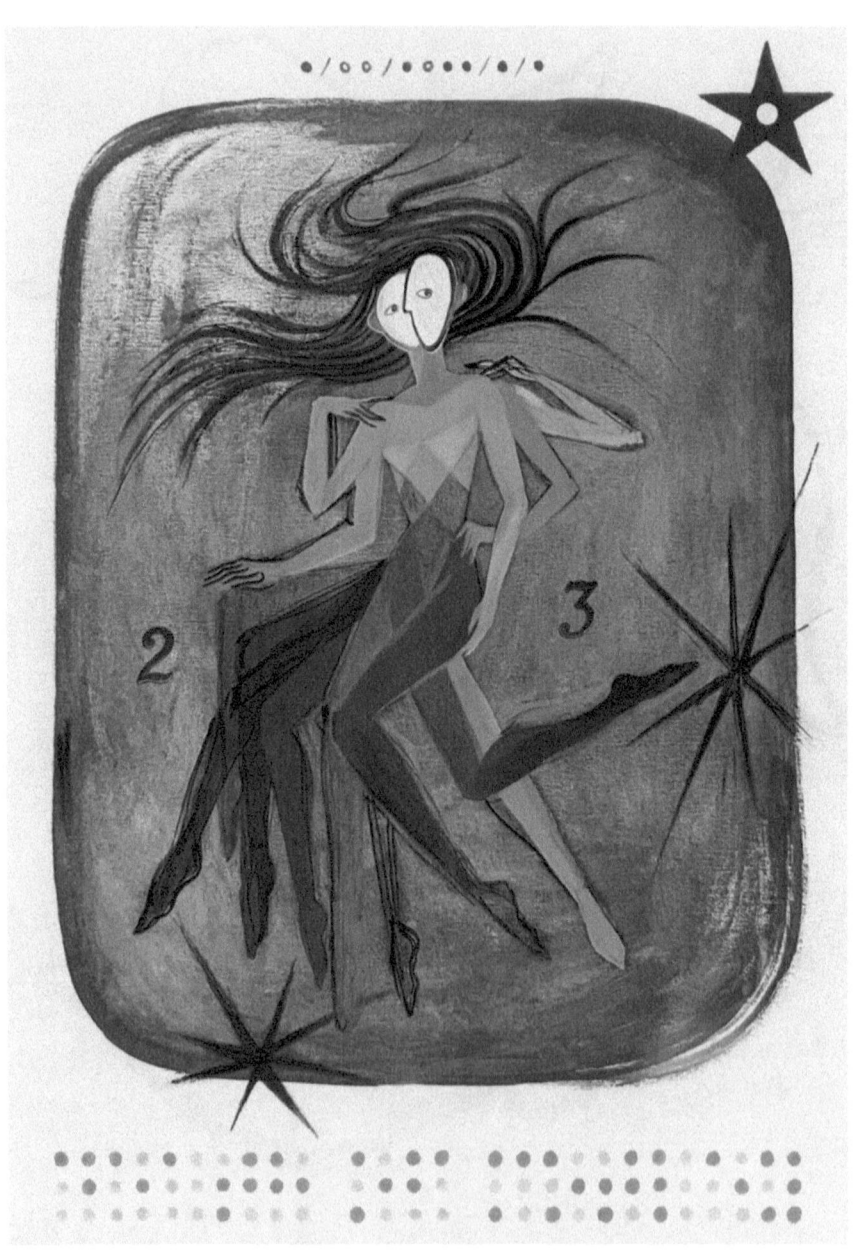

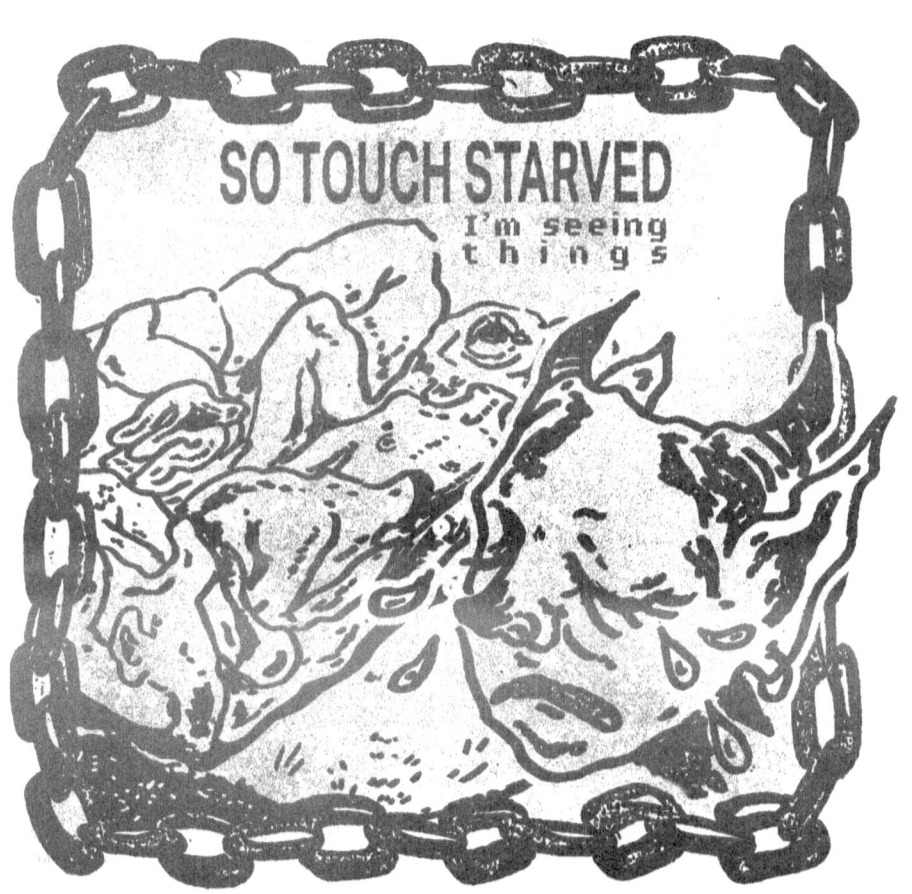

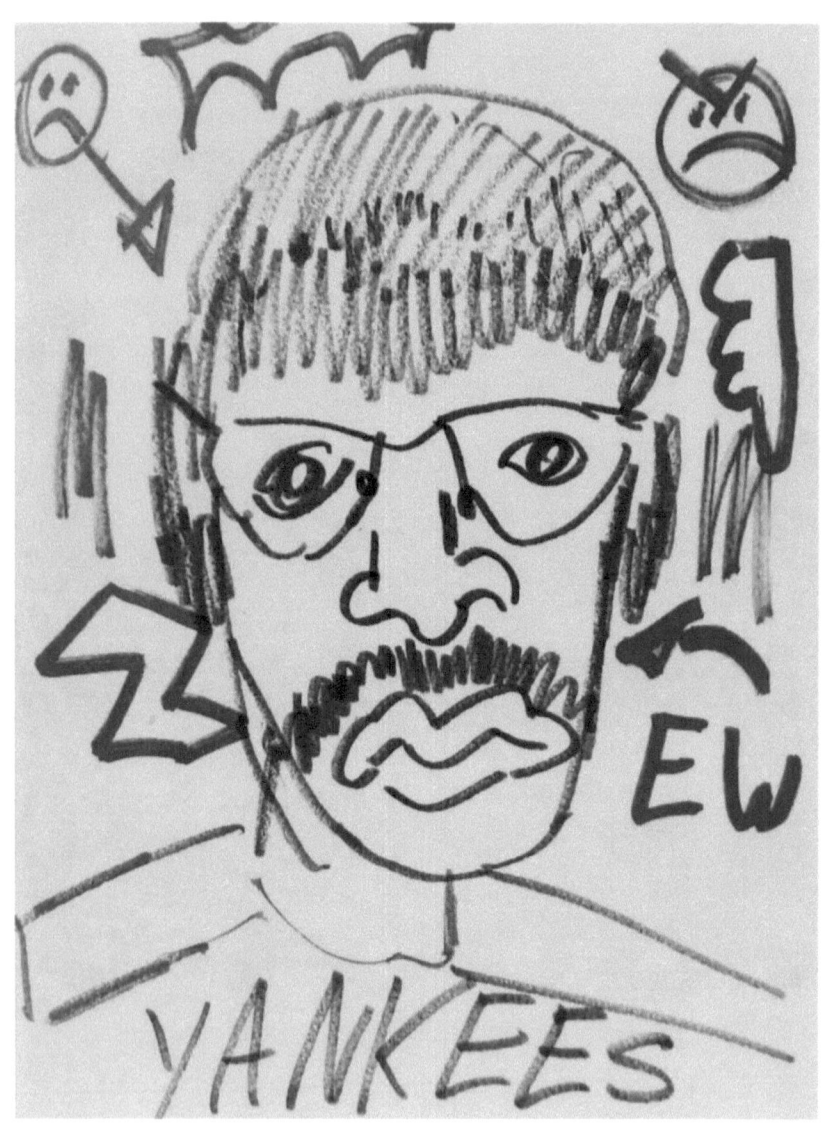

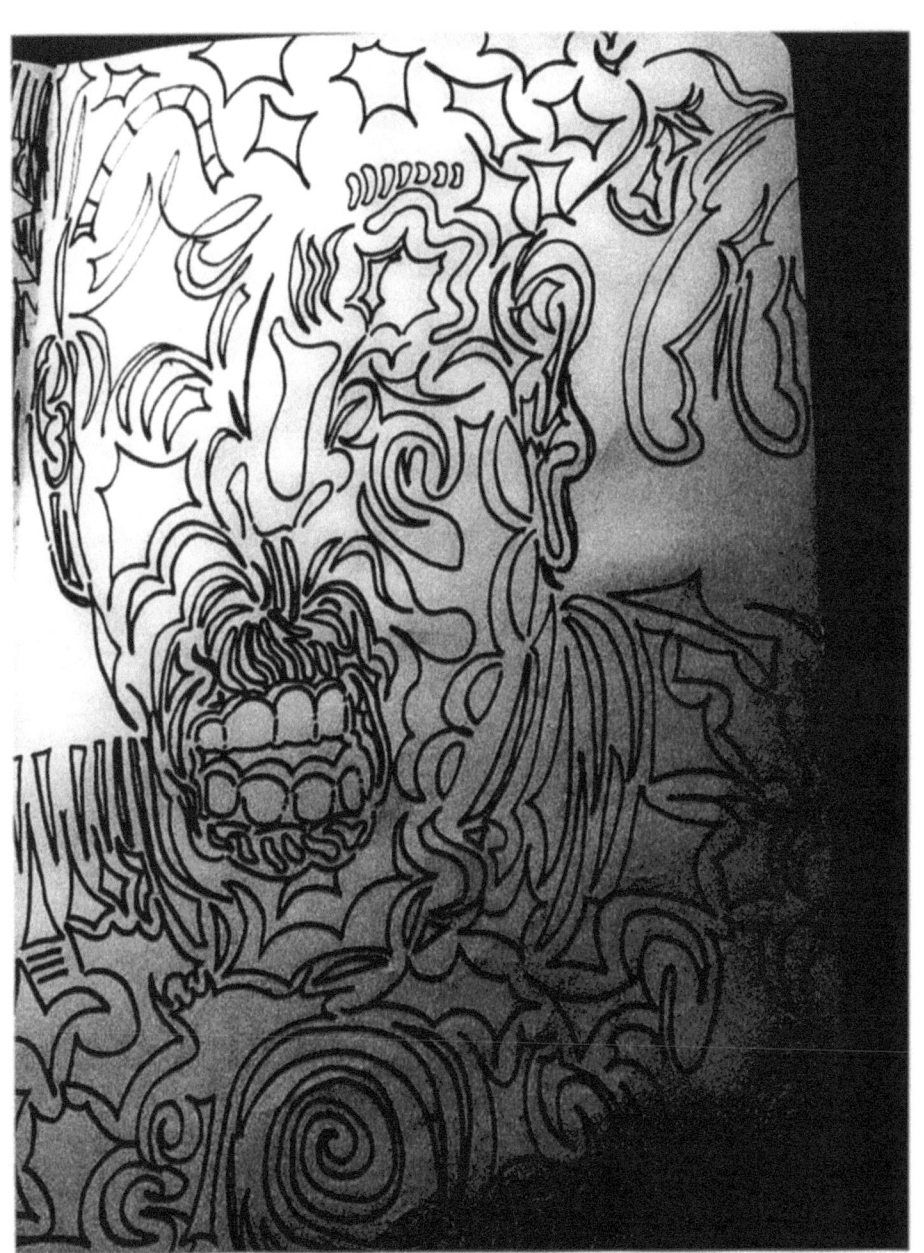

Rabbit's Foot

By multitudes of tunnel
I was lead here
to iron baskets of plenty
gathered from the edges
of the overflowing
mouths of well clad demons
I do not barter with,
but simply thieve from
their stock of discards
marked for burial
in some distant mound.
Look Away, look away
you shall not see me
forever vanishing
forever young.
Your elden friend,
their forgotten face.

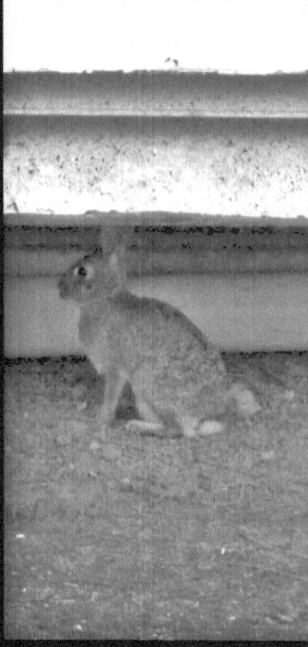

(Lepus Pergamentum')

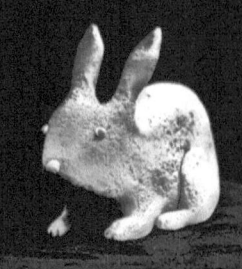

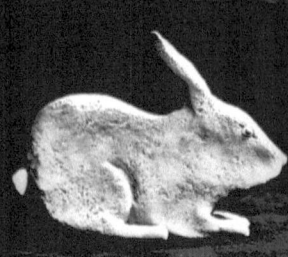

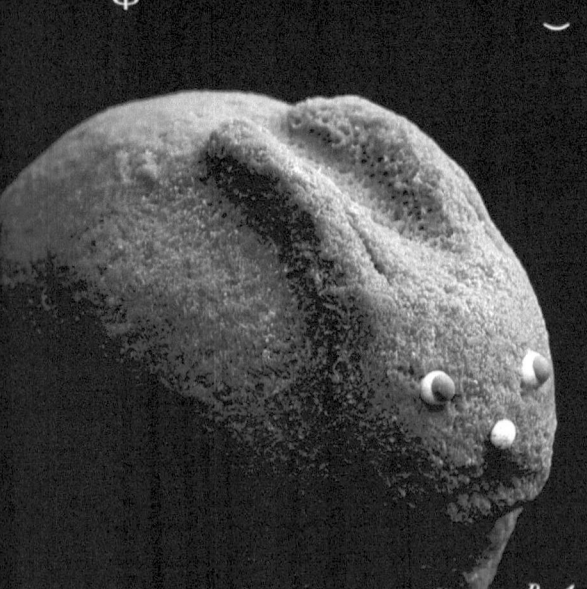

BARDO BREAD

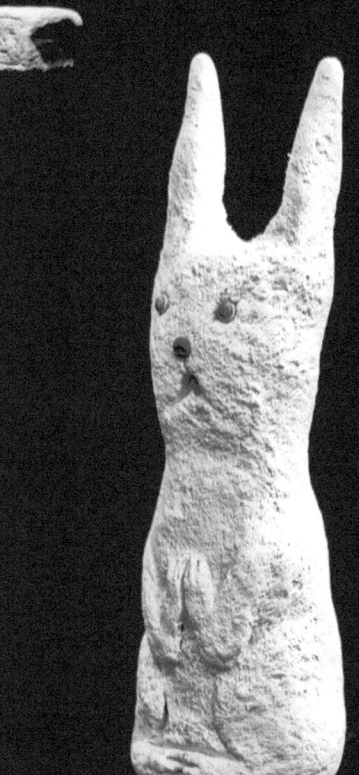

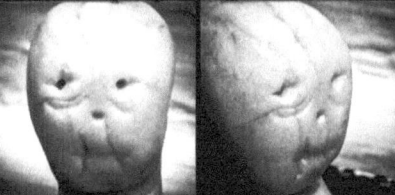

look into my daughter's eyes

and tell me nothing is sacred

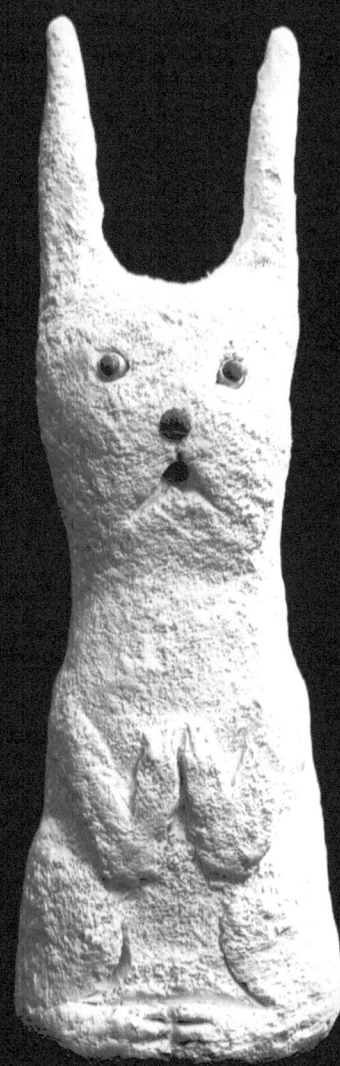

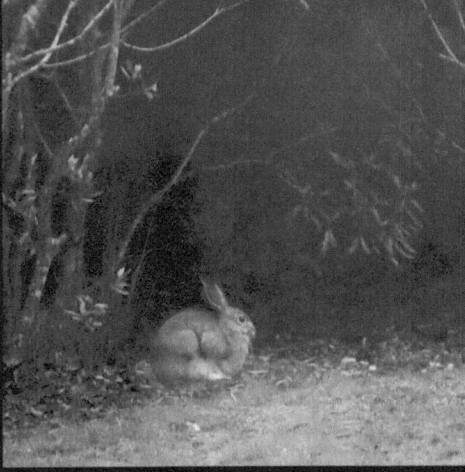

(Lepus Ferus³)

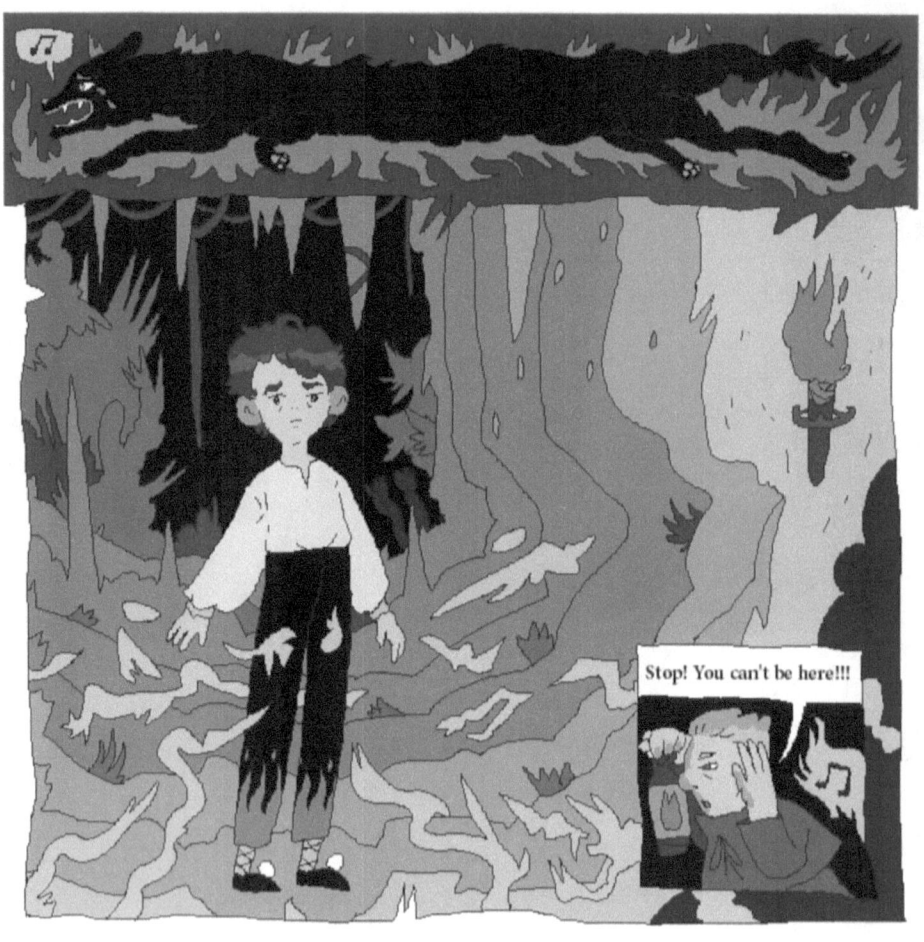

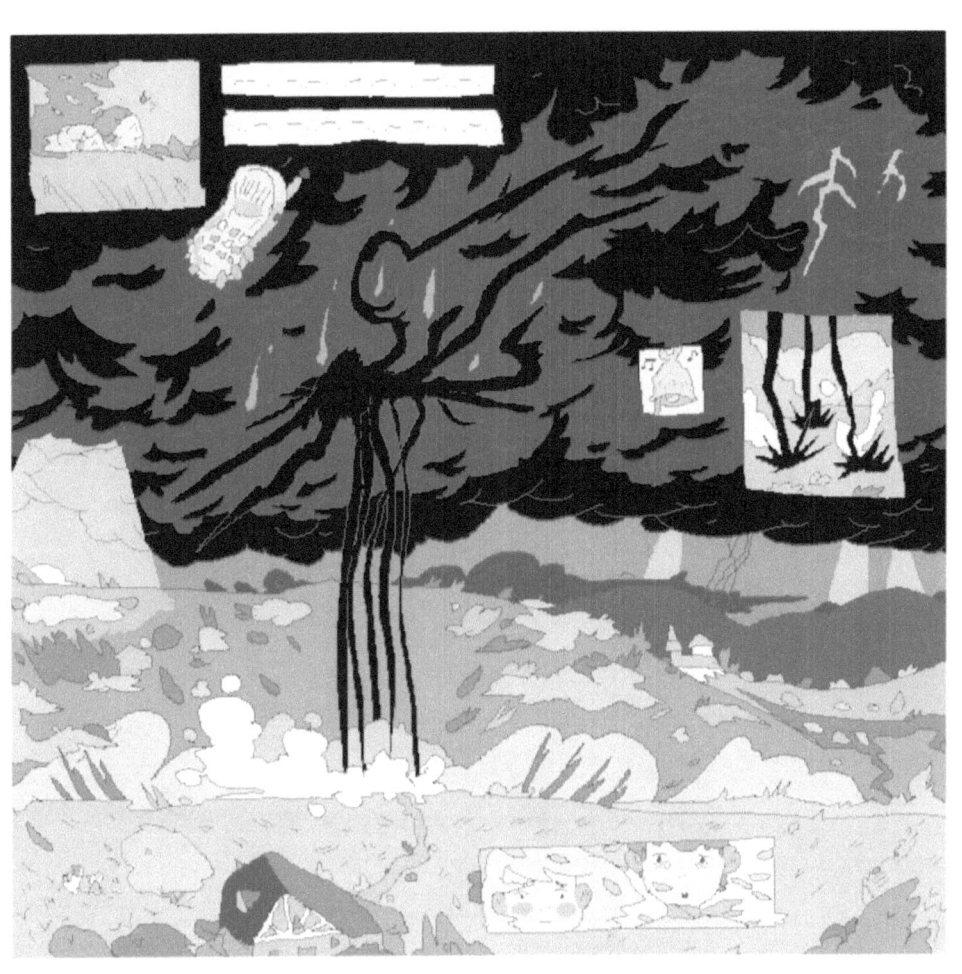

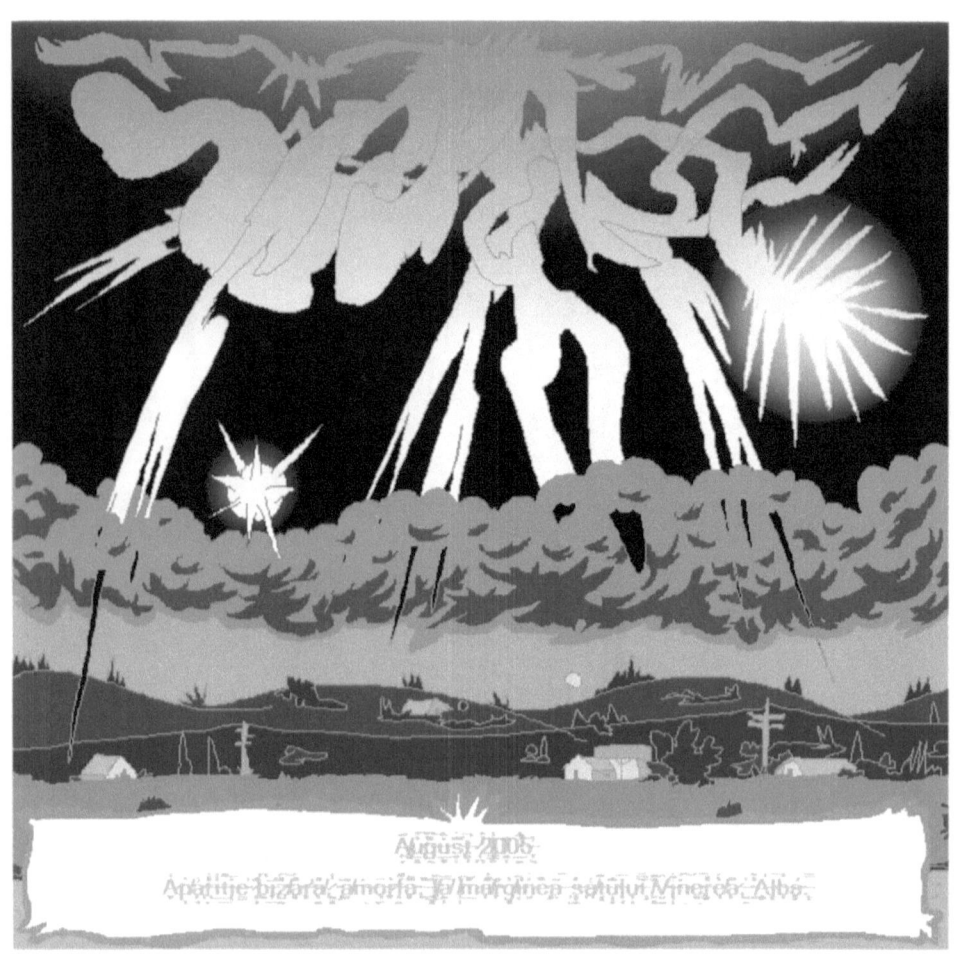

August 2006.
Apariție bizoro- amoro- în împrejurea satului Mircos Alba.

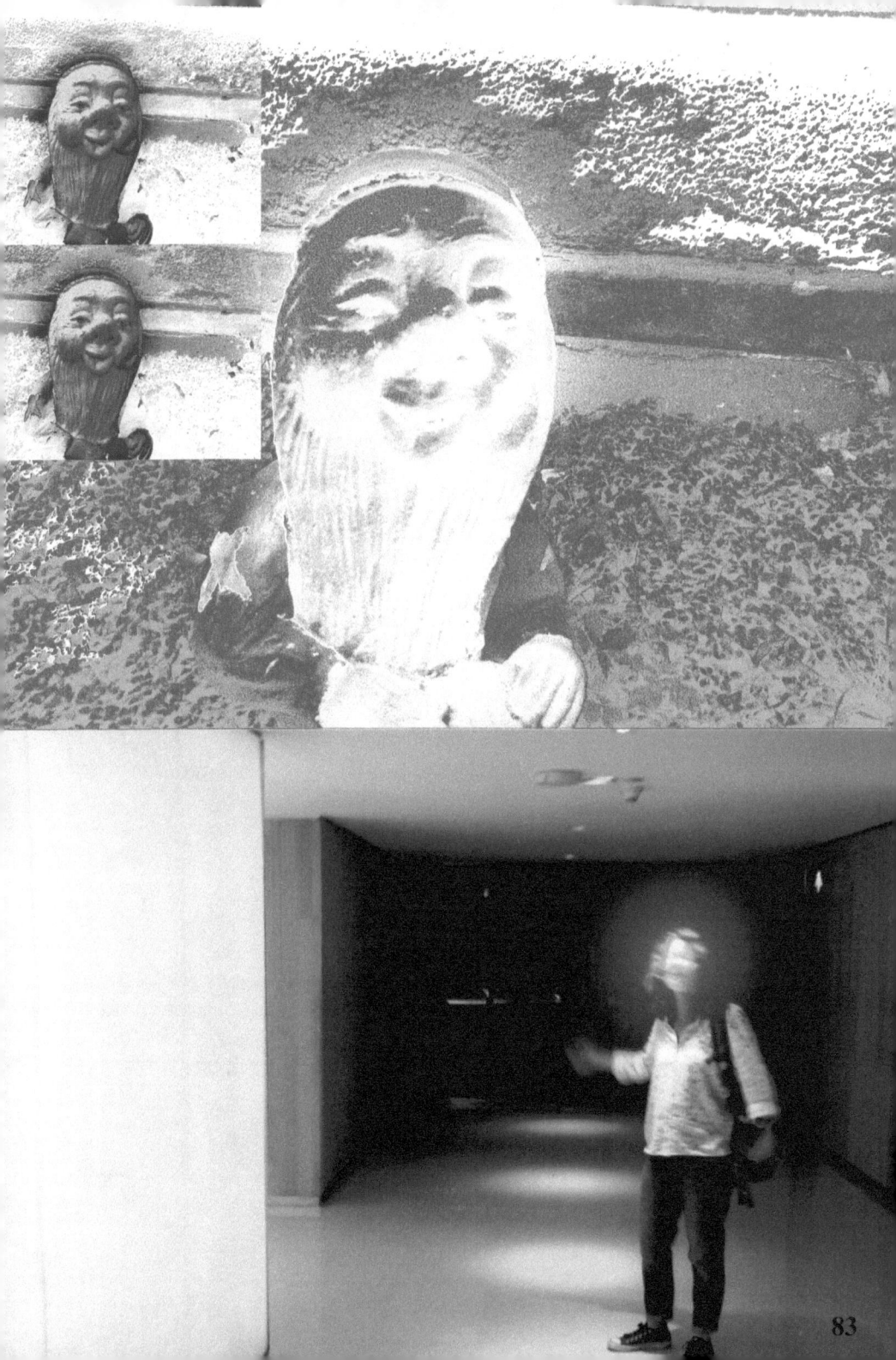

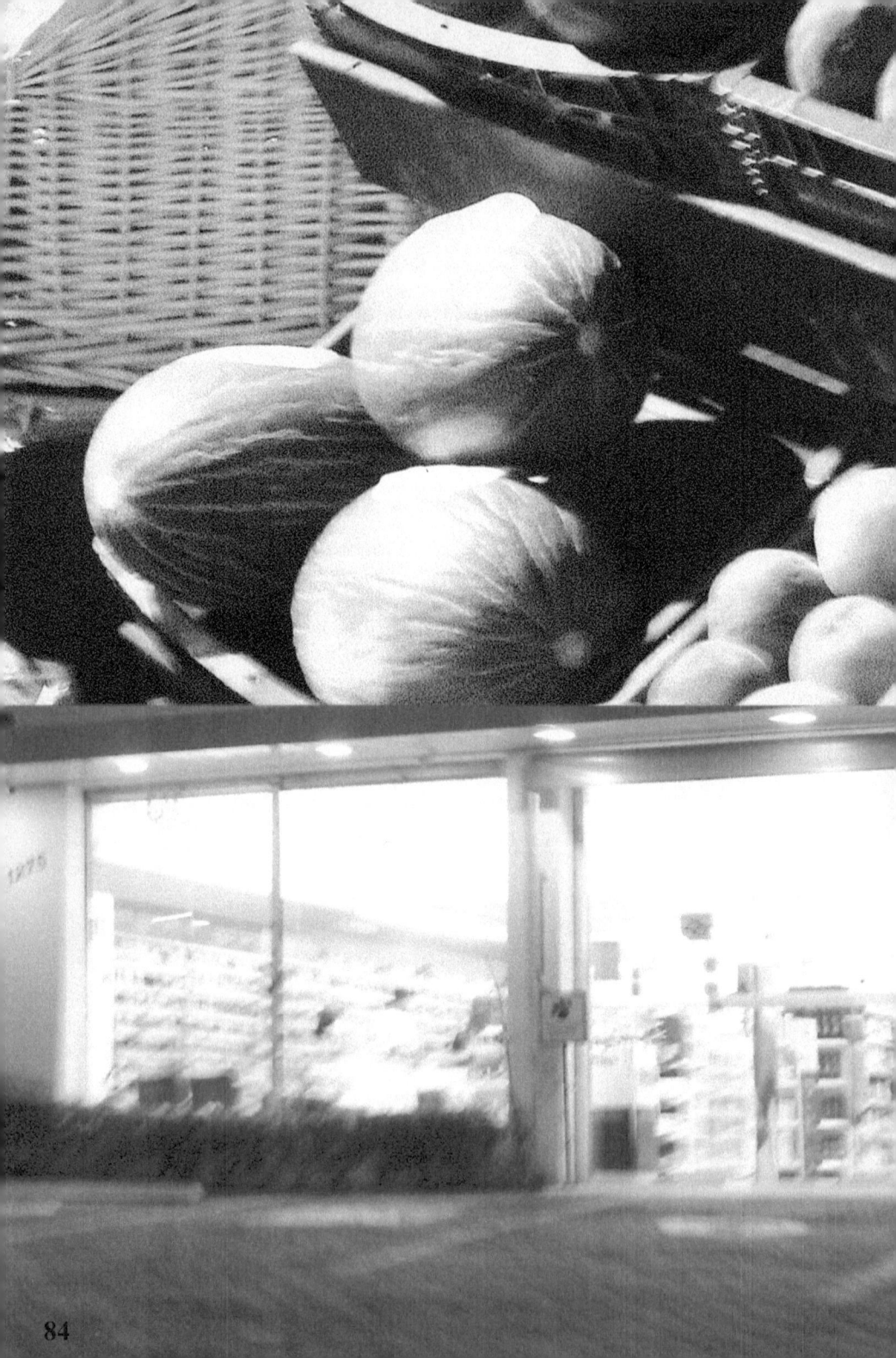

A SKY OF OYSTERS

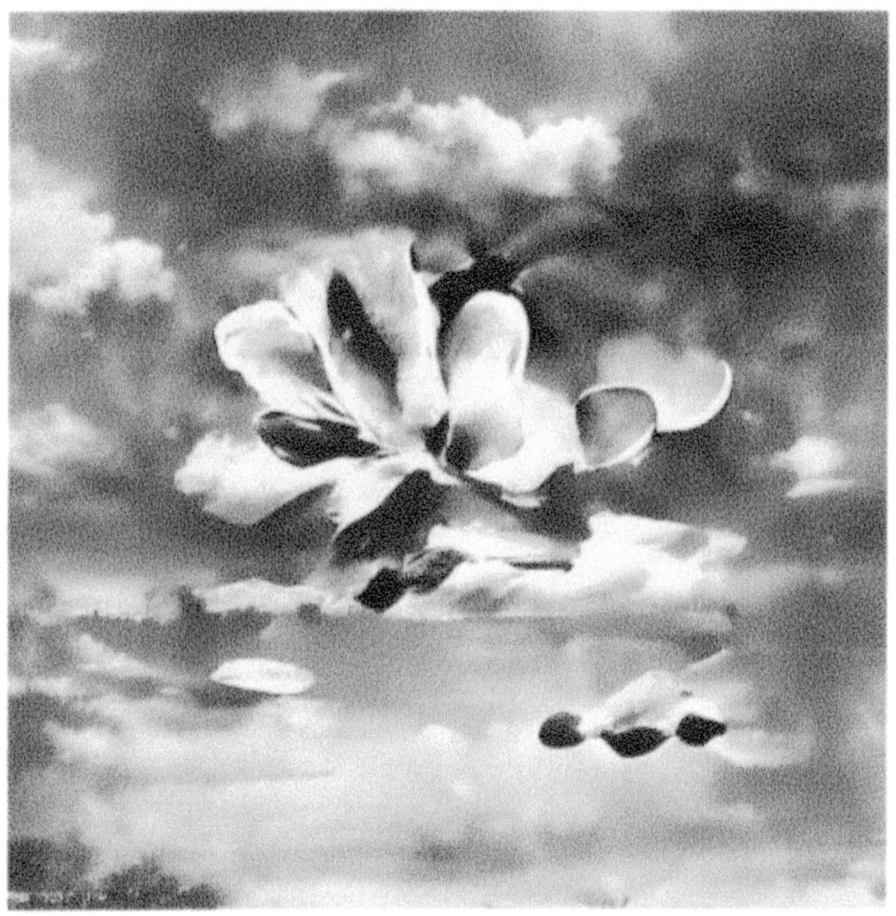

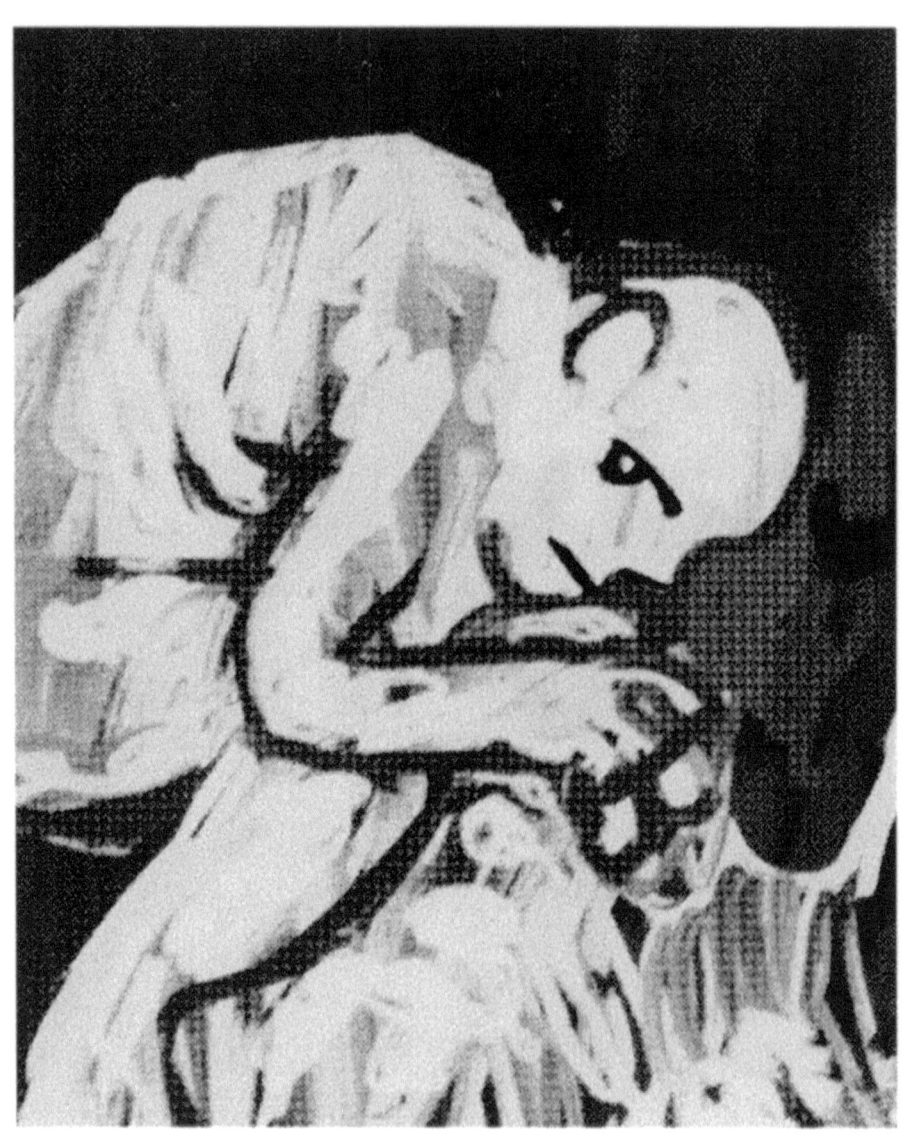

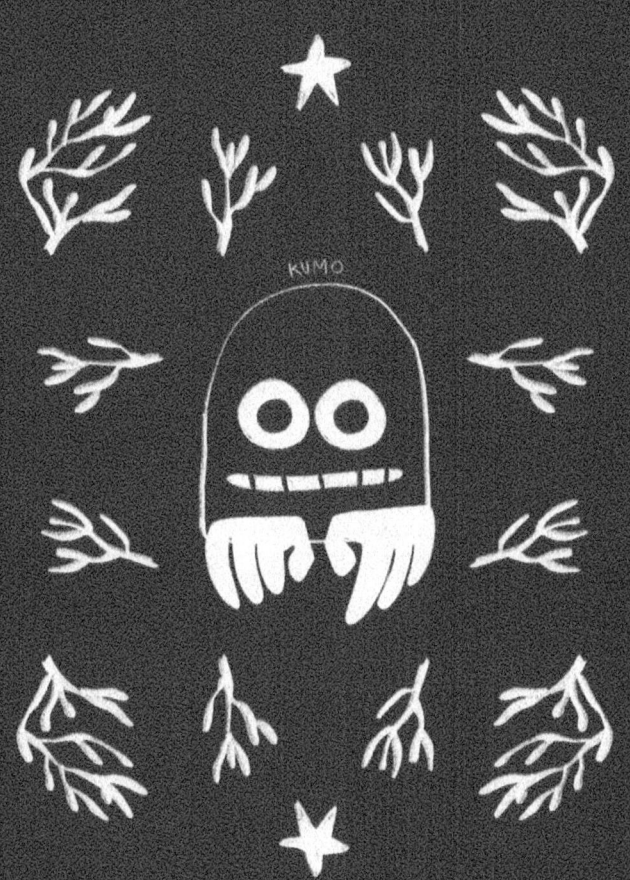

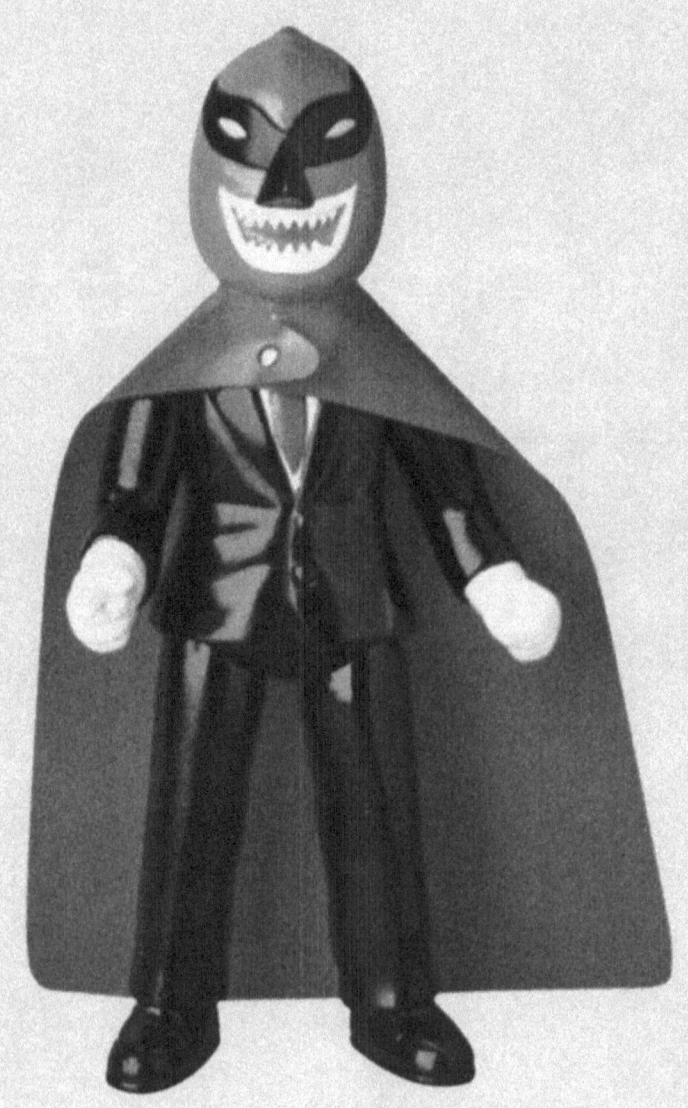

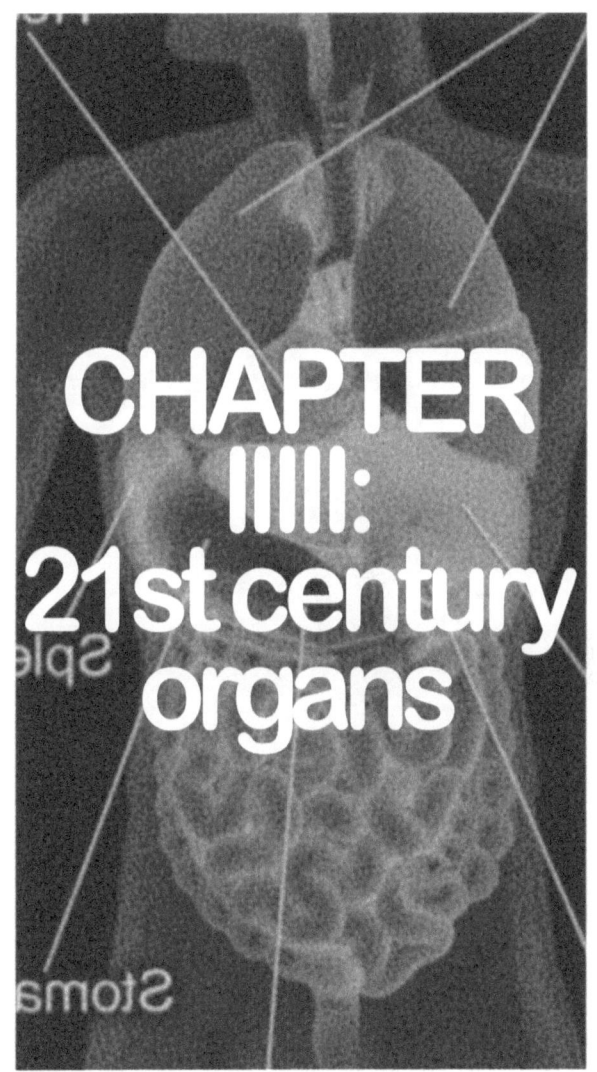

CHAPTER IIIII:
21st century organs

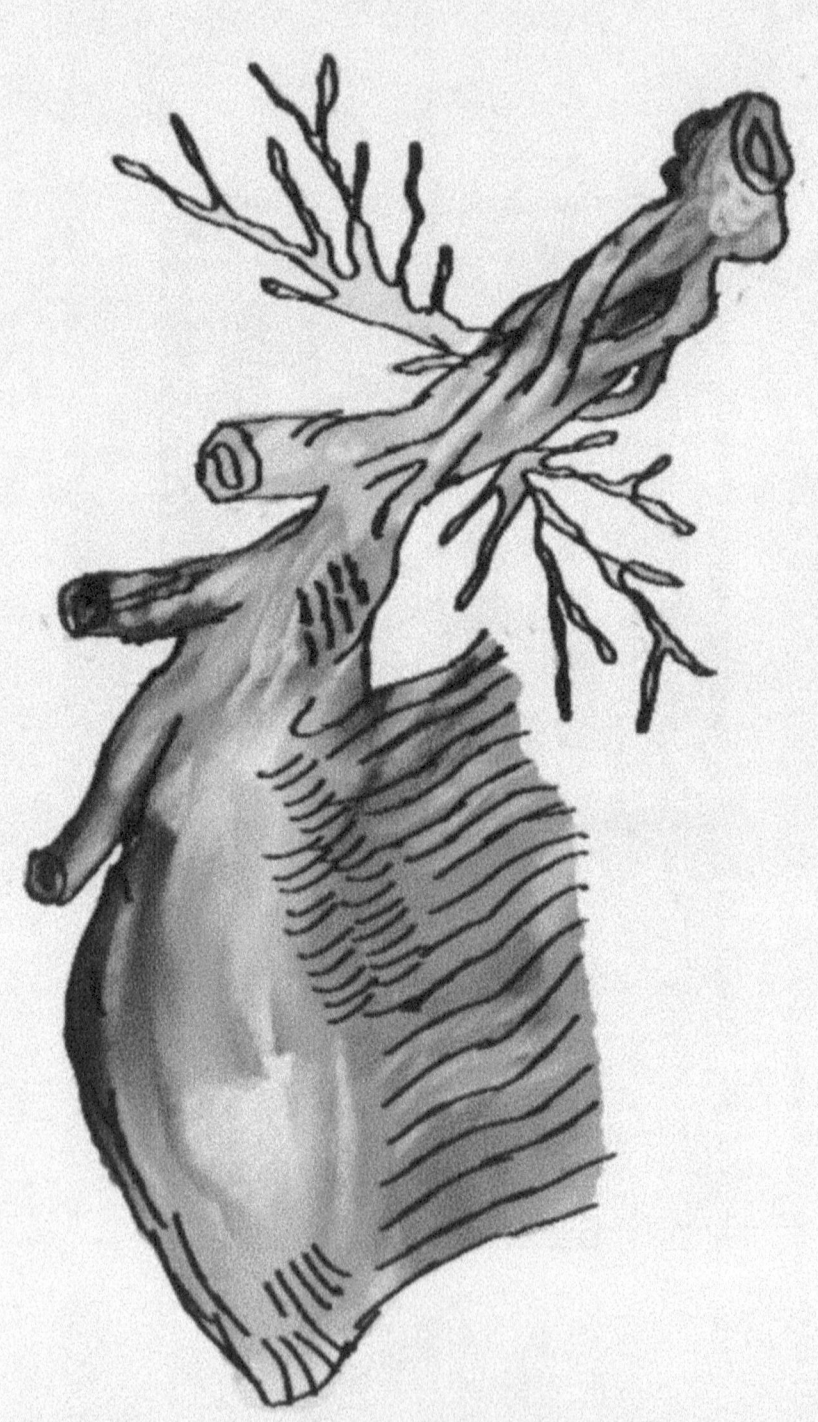

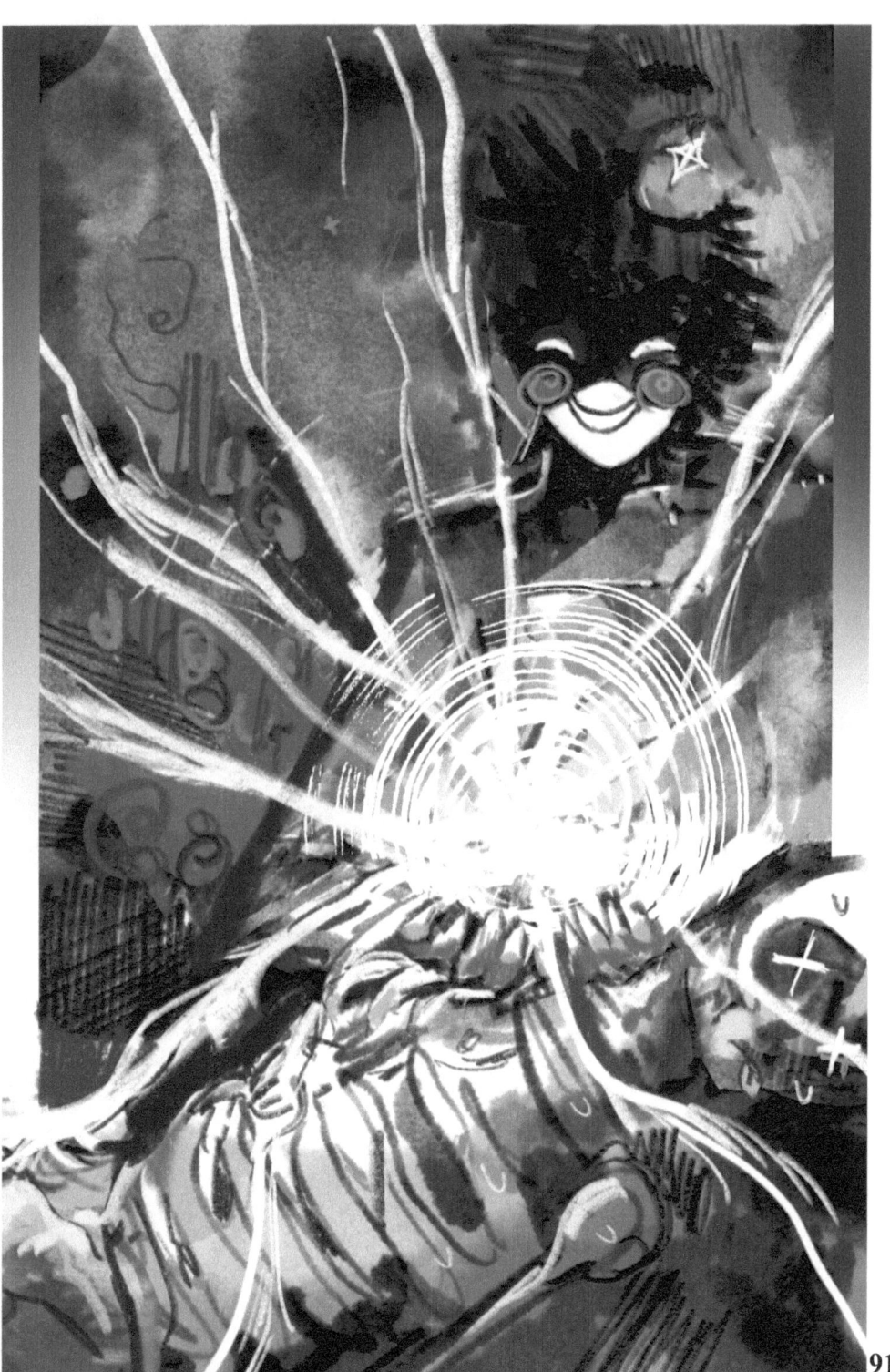

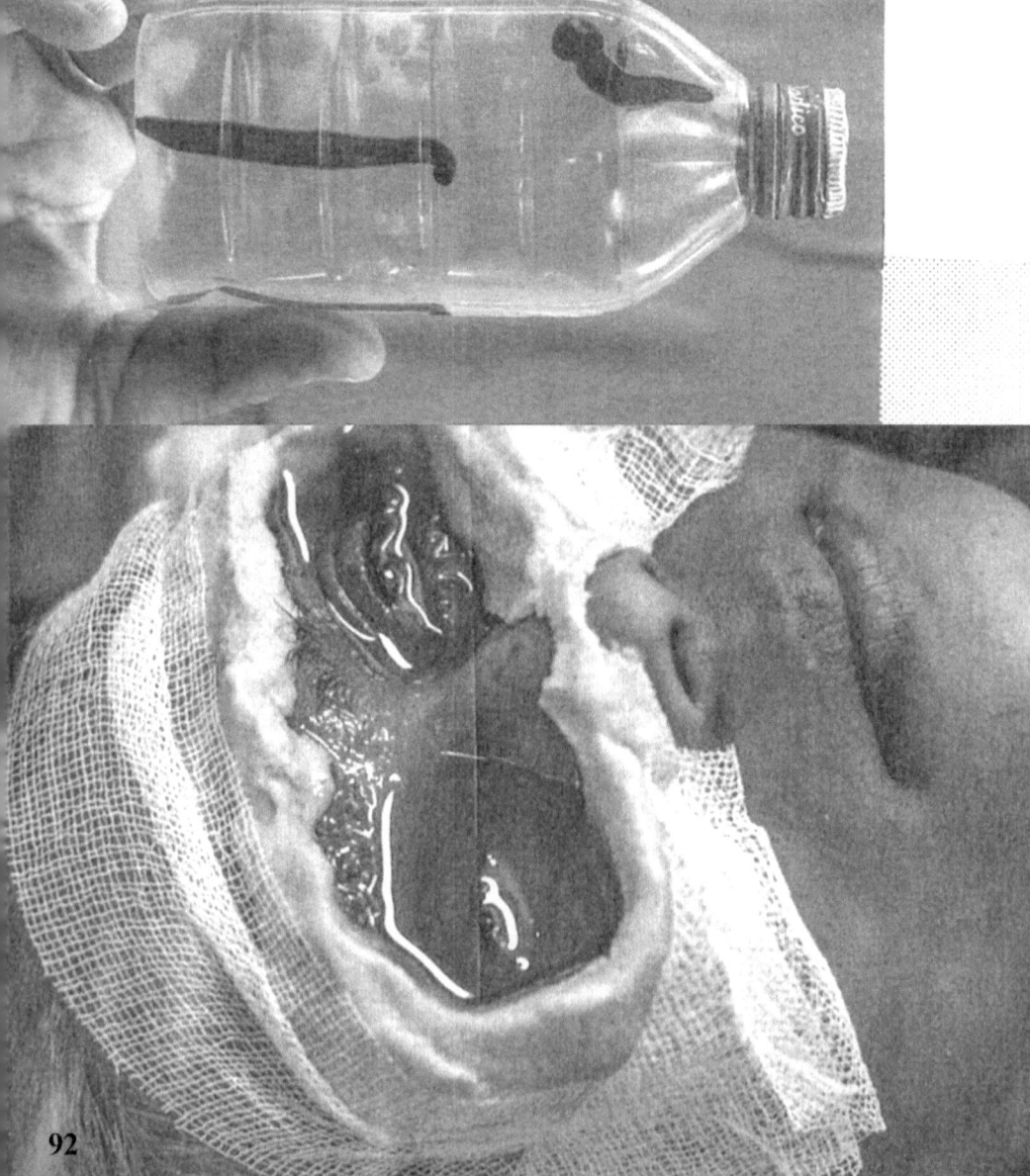

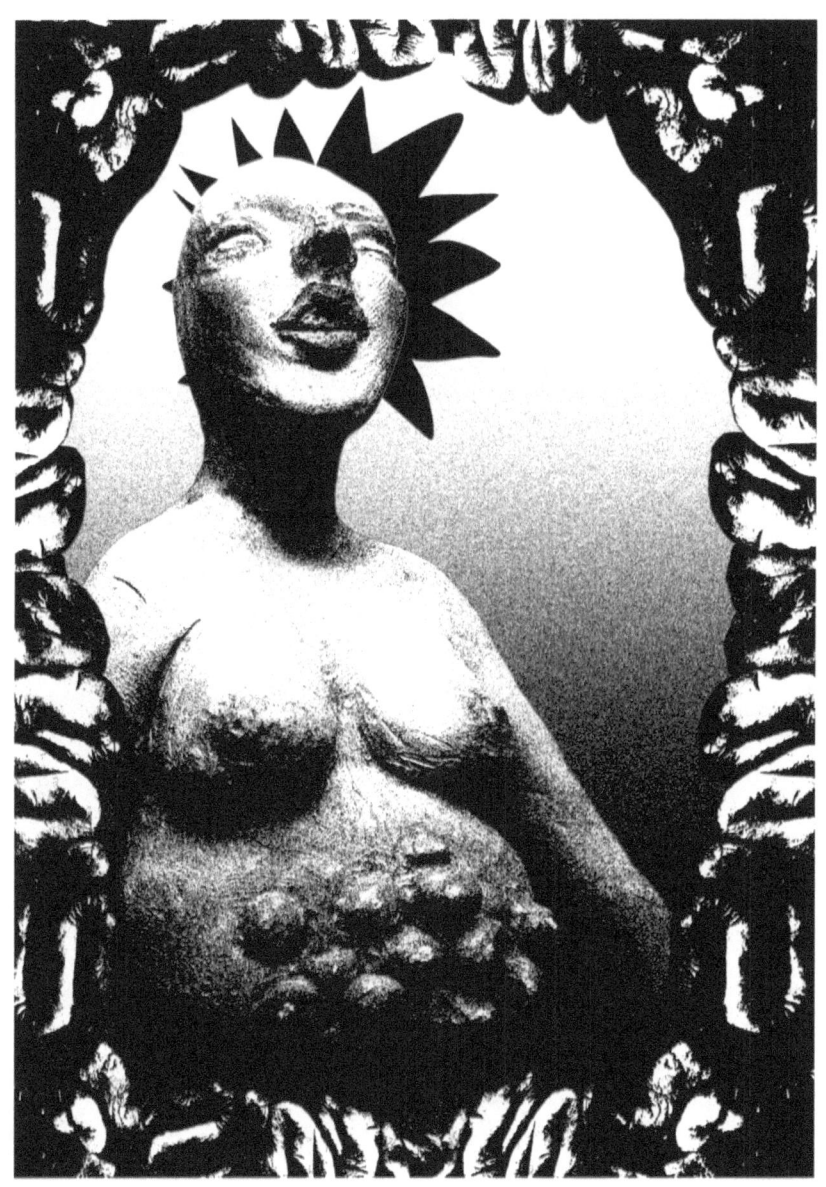

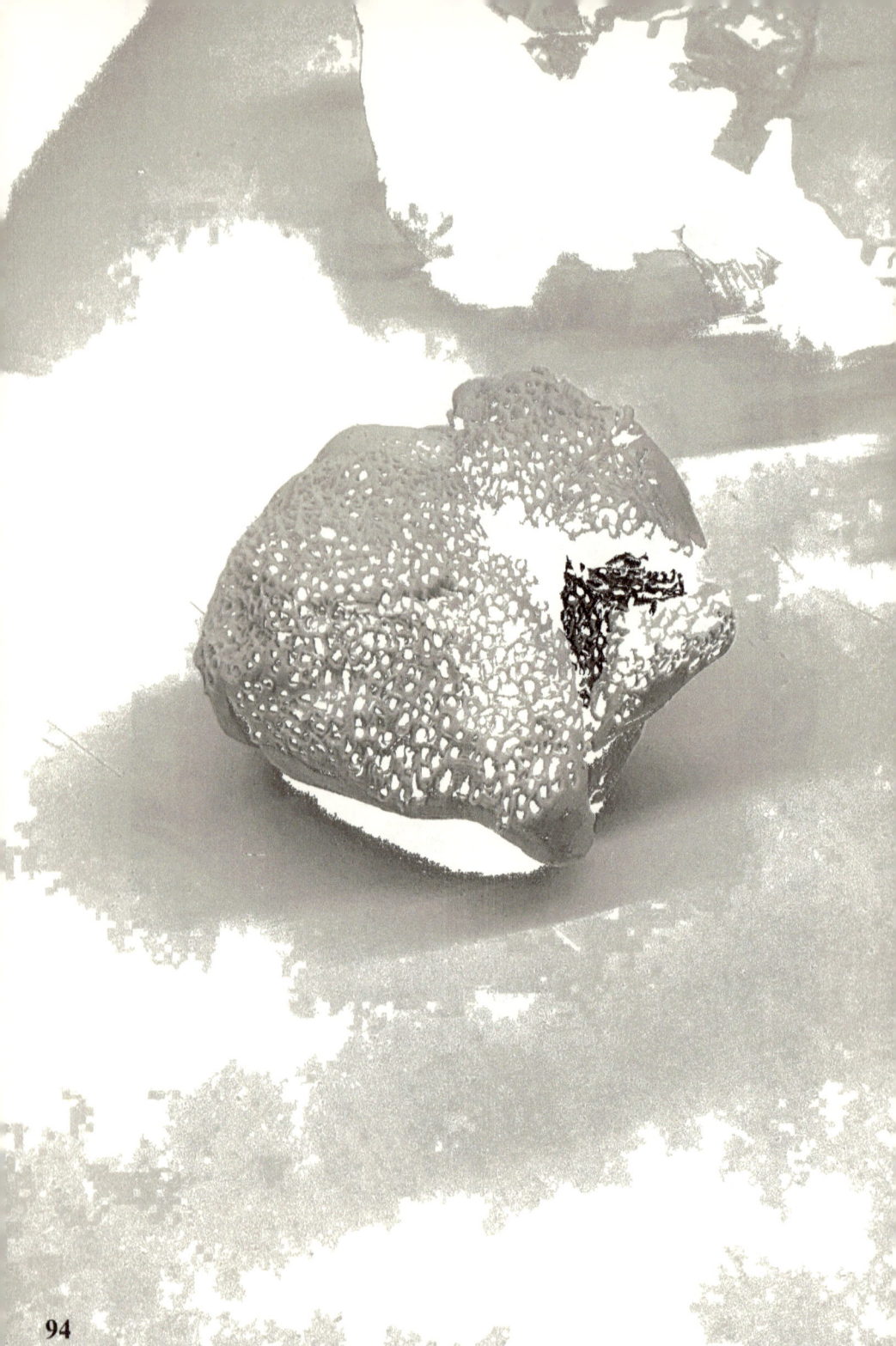

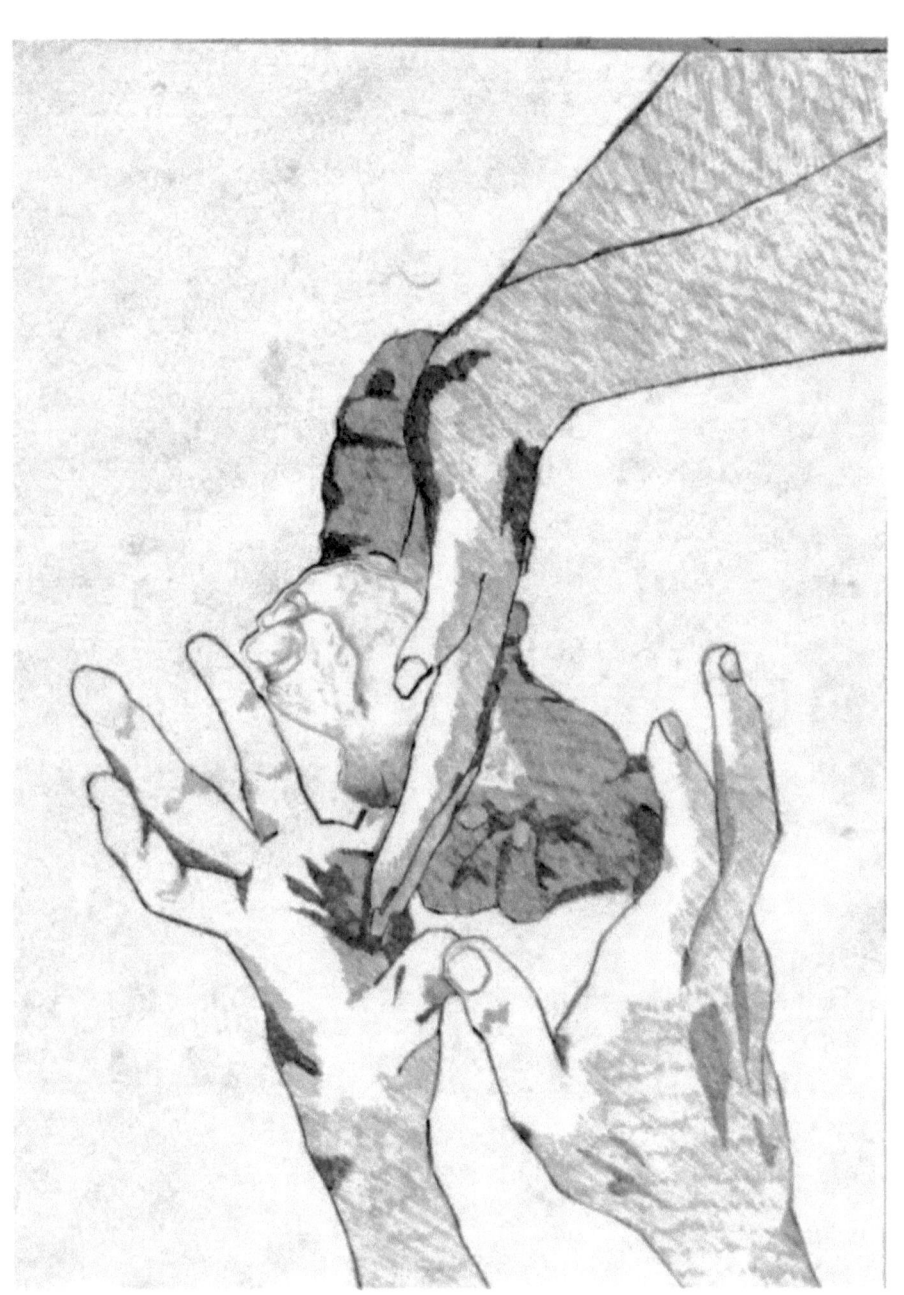

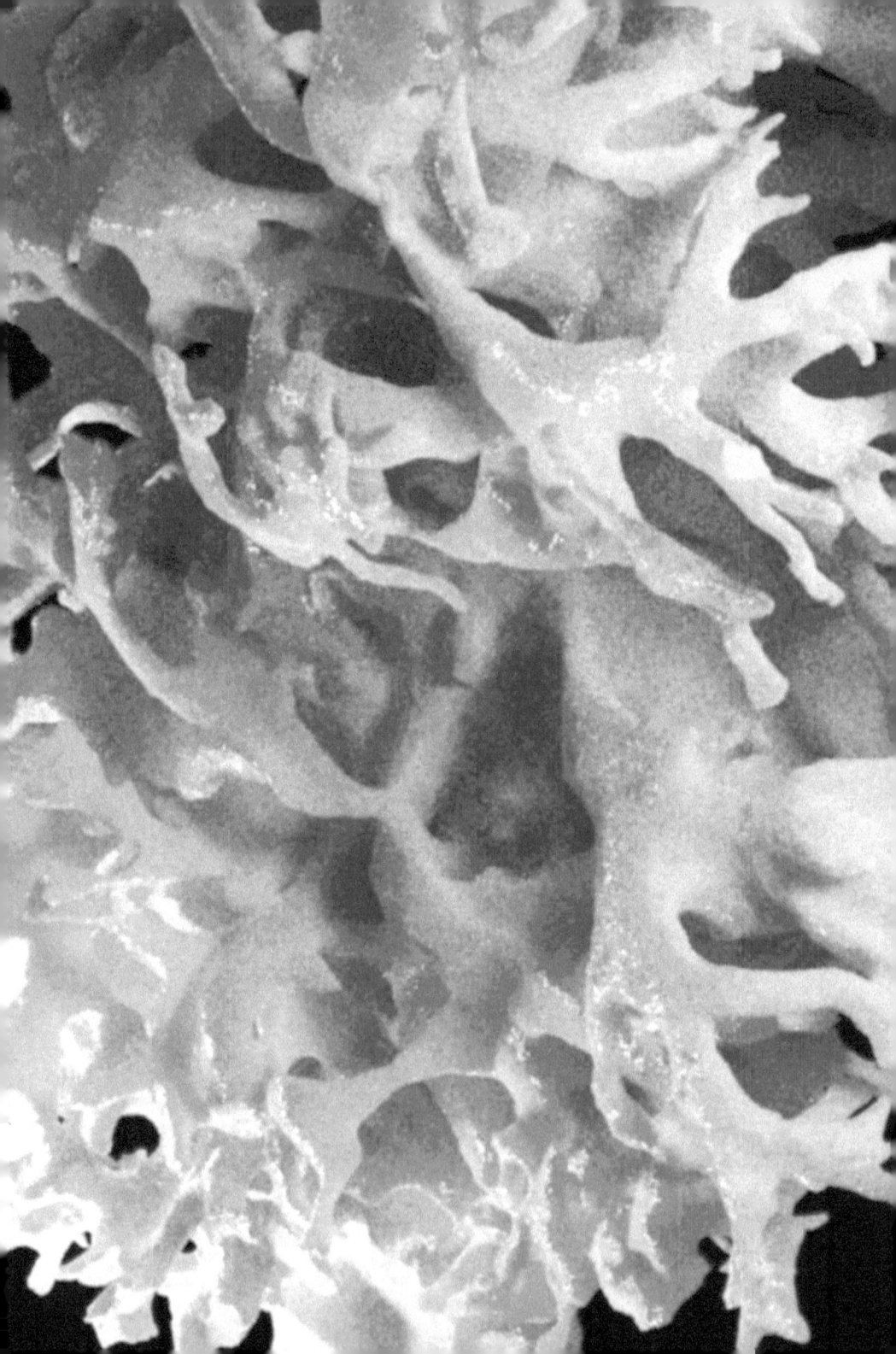

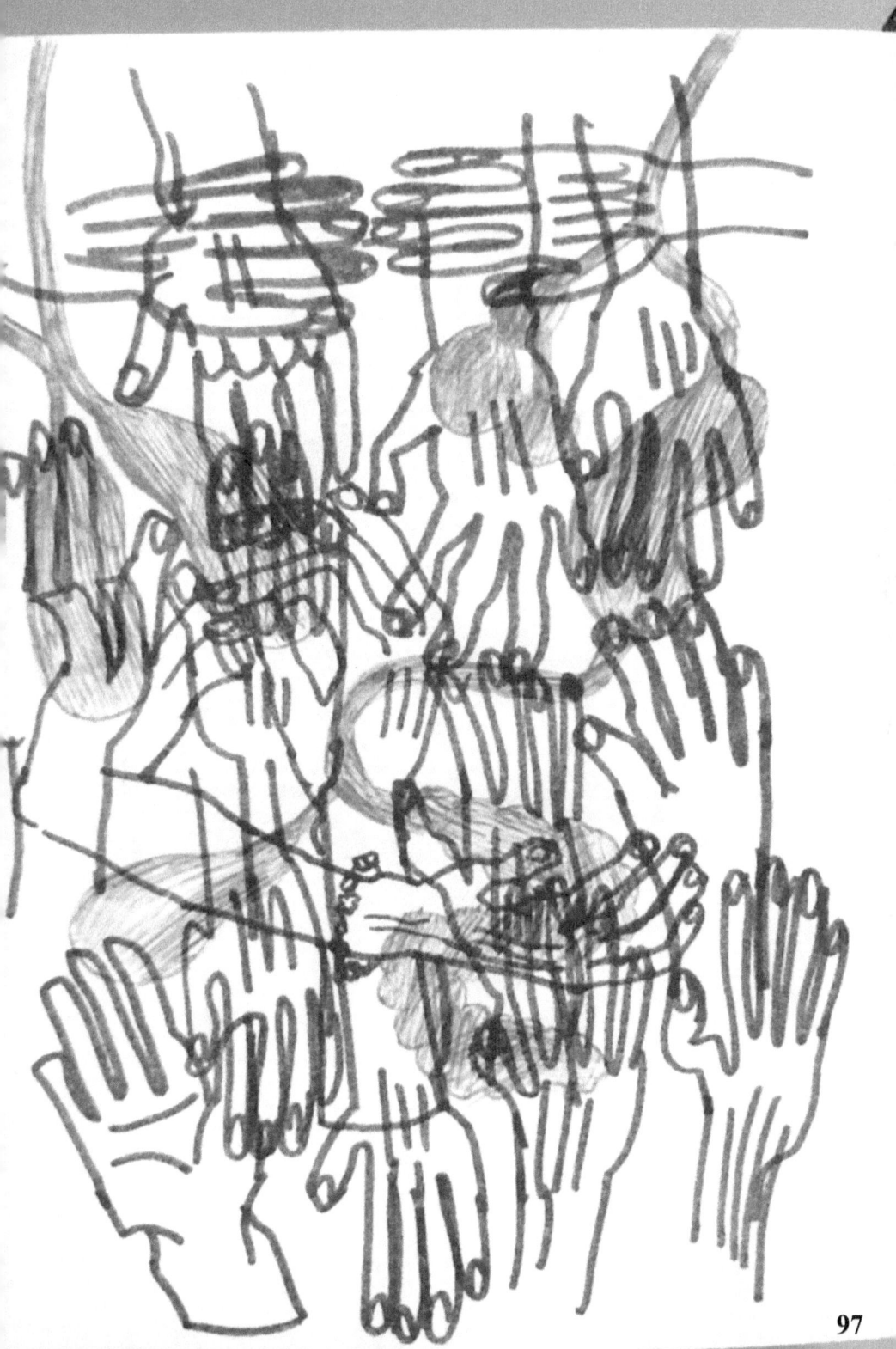

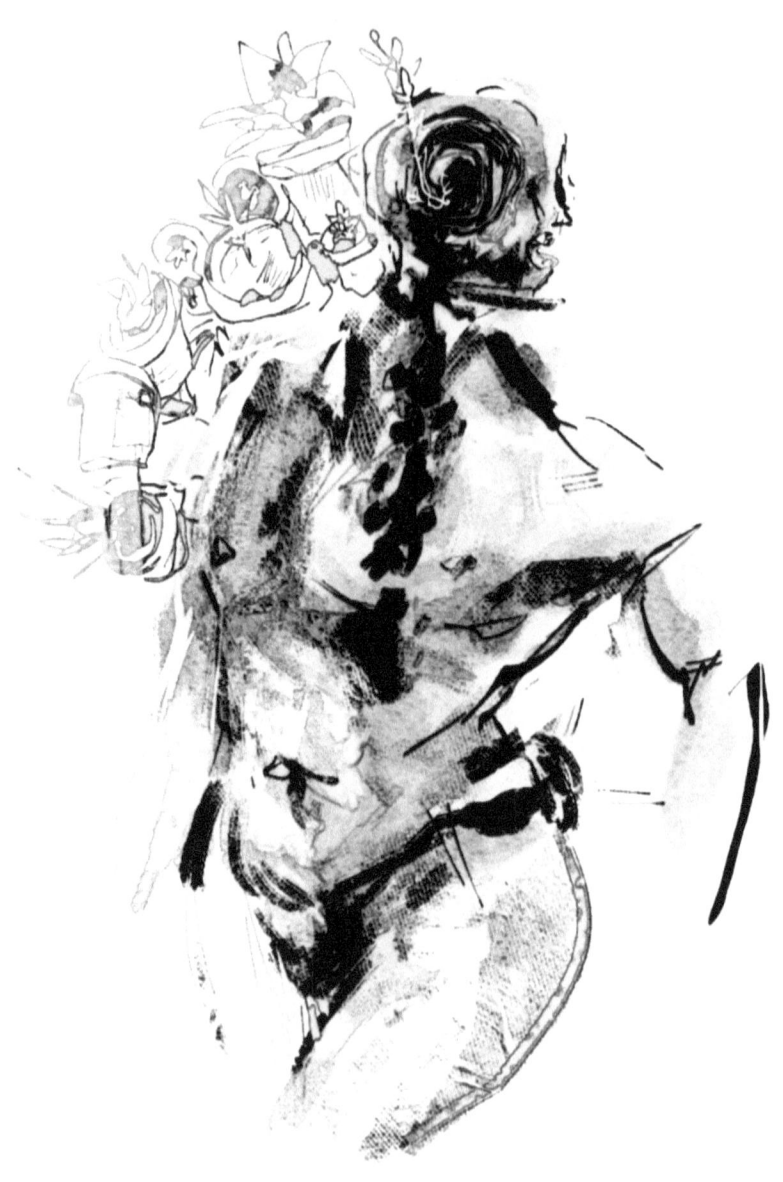

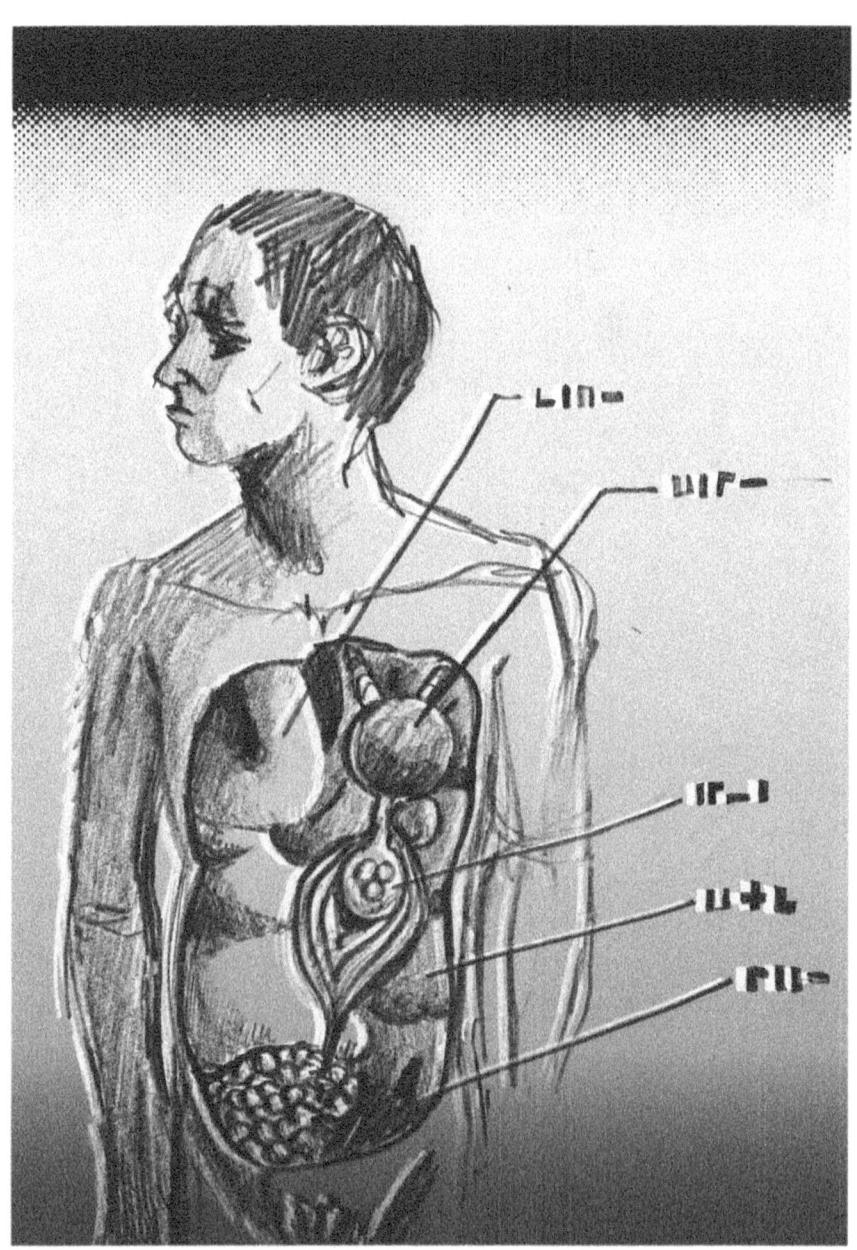

theFace
designed by Neocorpus®

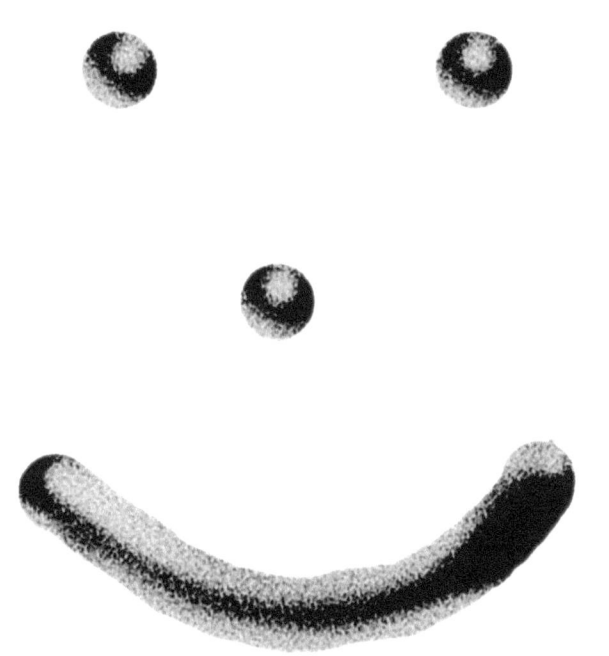

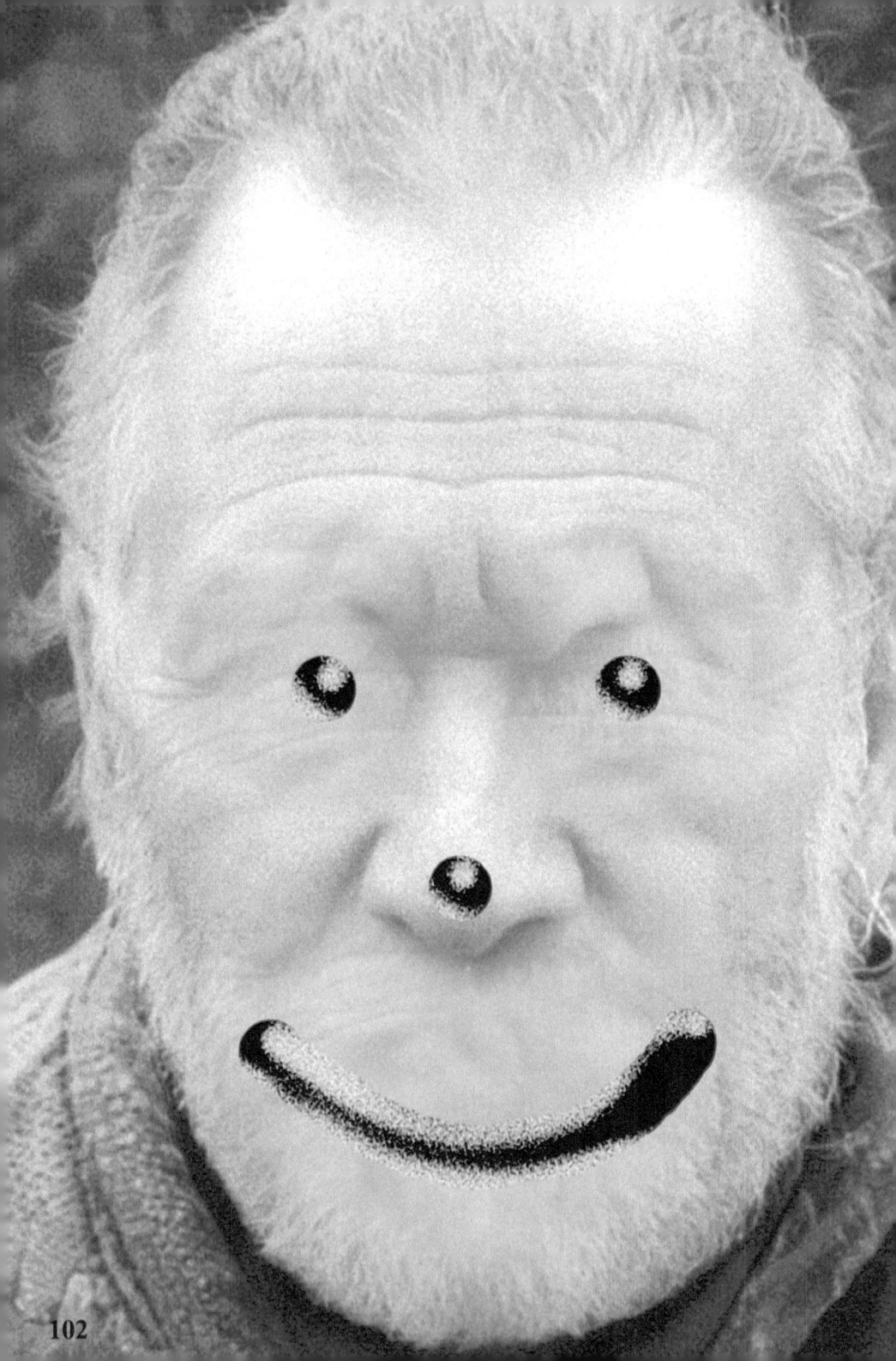

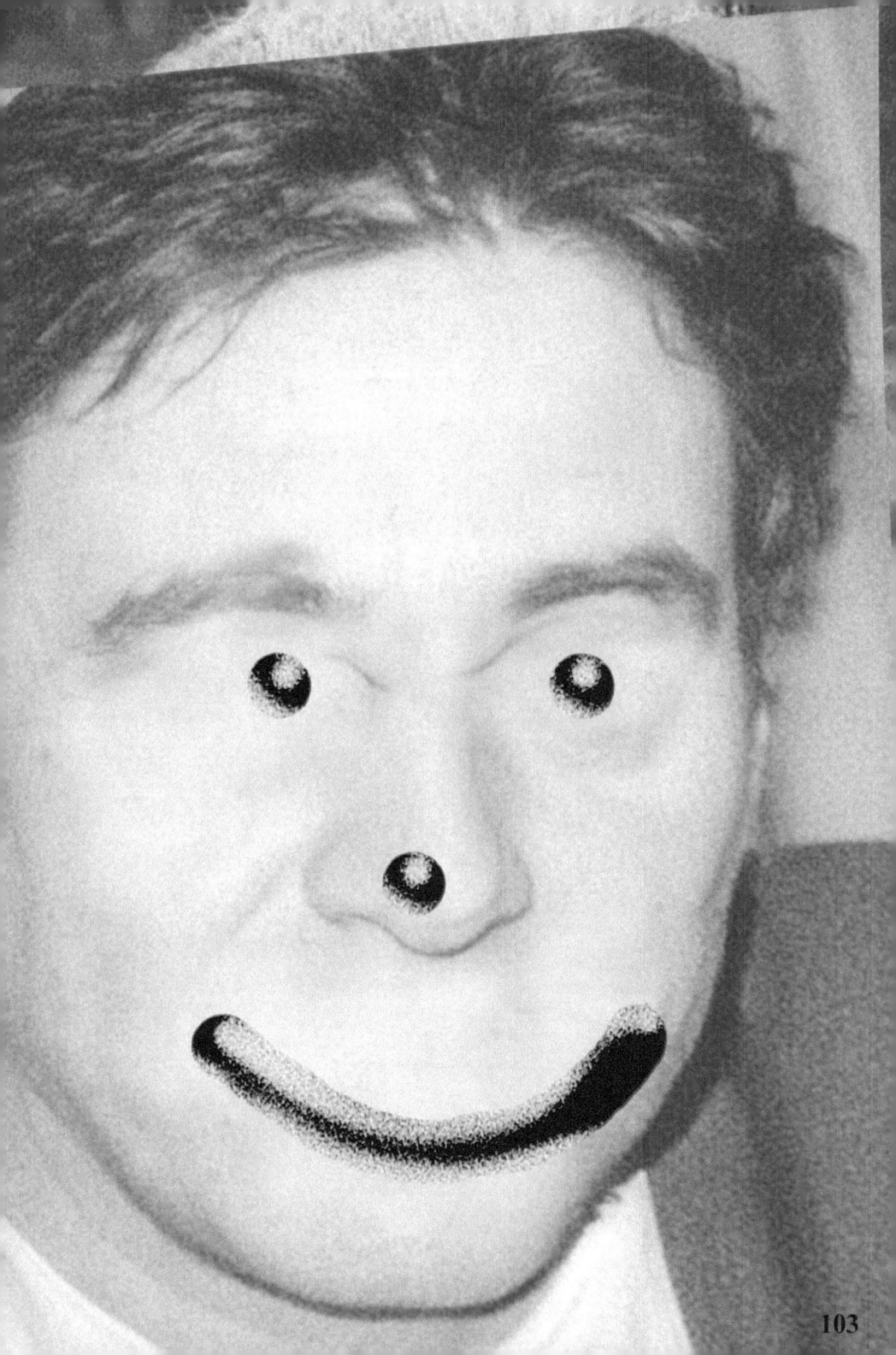

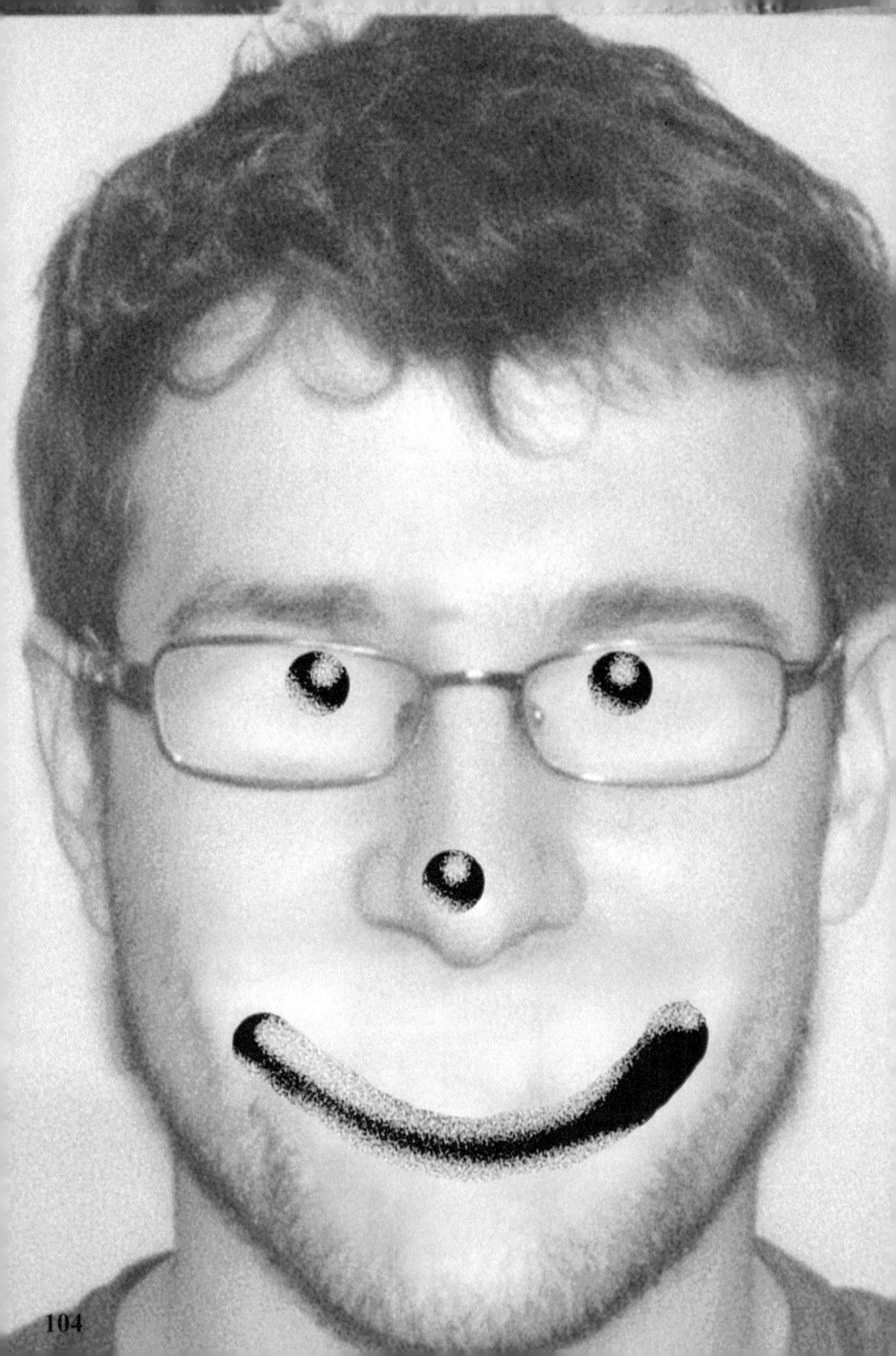

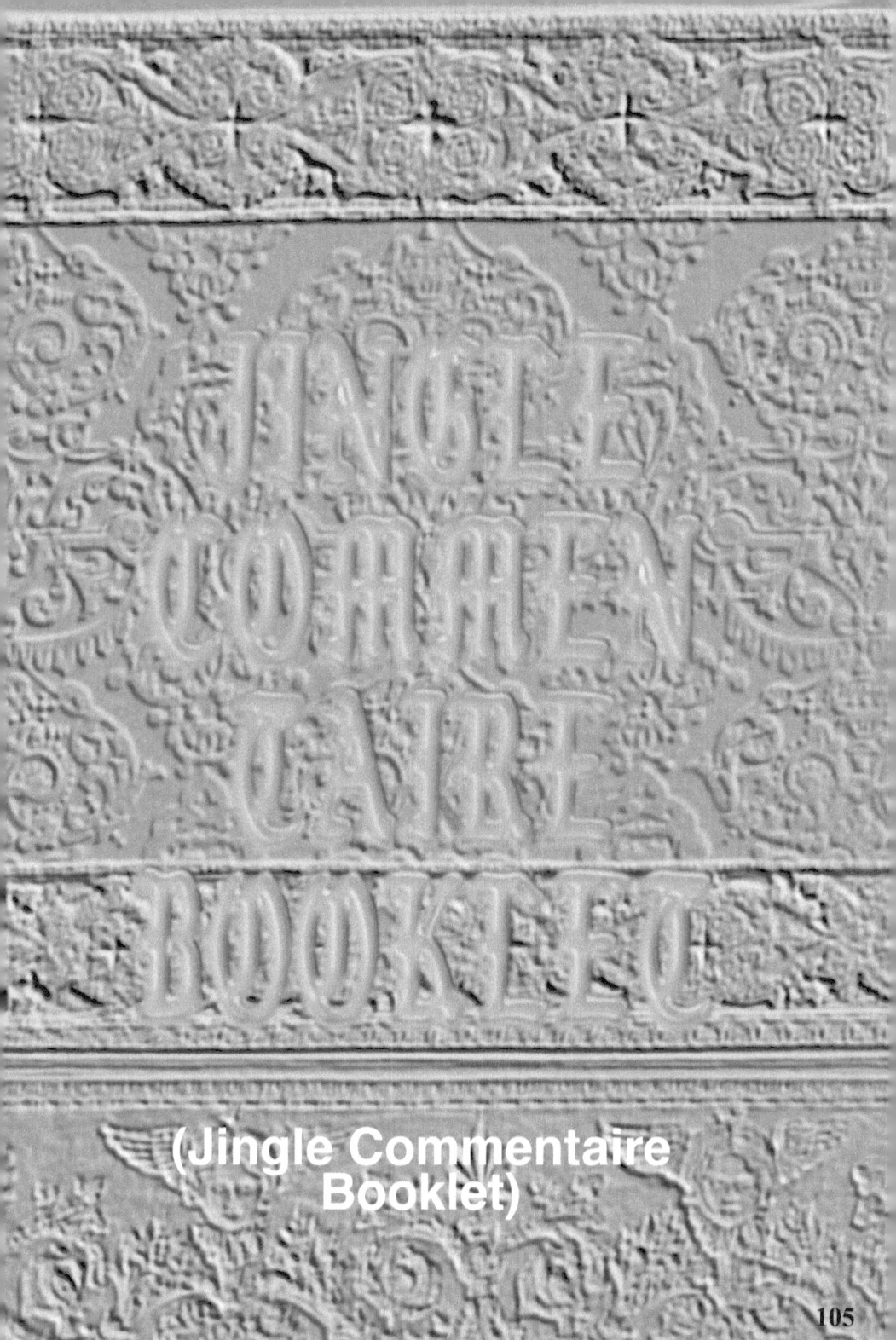

(Jingle Commentaire
Booklet)

Music stuff

Blutt (Patrick Belaga, 2021) review by Jorge

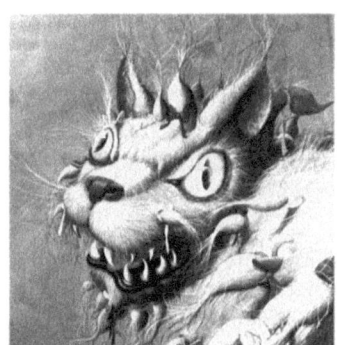

blutt, or...

...a digital cloud of self sleeping in a dark dreamworld, the photoshop blue sky, vast and open with dark clouds rolling through, not night but deader than night somehow.

patrick belaga's blutt is an anomaly. this album will make you see stars.

the cover of belaga's sophomore album is a seussian nightmare close-up of a candy-toothed cat with its fur tied off in festive bows. the name is german for "blood", perhaps a nod to the vivid red backdrop of this cat's universe, a dimension of thick, sludgy electronic cello that brings me back to nights as a kid waking up at 3am into the jelly of morning.

this freakish feline oughta have a pretty nasty purr, huh? well, blutt is belaga's attempt to capture that humming, stuttering motor. he embodies this cat in the album's 37-minute runtime; the coarseness of the fur, its vacant, angry stare, the calcium powdery touch of its bared teeth.

compared to 2017's groundswell, the foreboding is more subdued. if that album was being trapped inside a mountain vortex, this is being lost out on a snowy plain. don't get me wrong, there's still an ancient feeling here, but the watery production feels more ephemeral than primal.

belaga wastes no time putting us at the center of this blizzard with the opener. cello is the first thing you hear on this album, and it's central to the cold you feel throughout, but what makes this album feel subzero is the sound design. under that gorgeous cello, there's an ominous twang signaling danger, trespassing, a pinprick tingle that you do not belong here.

a lot of the melodies on this record are simple repetitions of an idea. on sigh, a piano progression is established, eaten and then spat out in variations at different stages of digestion. the filtered recording feels close - too close, confined by concrete walls or the contours of a cave. the horn screeching is an echo drawing in these disembodied hums that follow the chords for the rest of the song.

the ambient noises add motion. while listening, you feel a whirling wind, like a demented version of the dizziness from spinning too fast as a kid. except instead of the hard landing, you fall slow.

when i watched felix colgrave's double king for the first time, i felt sucked into another dimension. the tunnel is a tower's rhythmic synth and spacious cello recall that feeling of being a motionless observer. to me, blutt just sounds like night, those bright nights where the sun might still be out if it weren't asleep.

sleep is this album's crux, a restless sleep where belaga's compositions sandwich crisp orchestral cello passages between processed noise ripped from a dream.

album closer and centerpiece slowly, clocking in at 14 minutes as the longest song on the record, is a prime example of this: time loops, error noises collapsed into circular frequencies spin on the axis of a two-note piano melody. the chaos is seductive; it lulls you into its simulation and transfixes you in it.

this album is the metaverse embodied, the lonely whirring fan of a supercomputer left to rot. when the connection's severed, when it's time to wake up, the dream never quite leaves you.

much like this album hasn't left me.

imagine a snowy wasteland. there's a blinding light wherever you look, and angels are singing, but these angels aren't like the ones you know. they're a chorus of distant holograms plucking wires, playing a song with a lilt you don't recognize.

once the angels dissolve into the sky, you wander until you find yourself shaking off the snow packed into your boots under a porch you don't remember walking to. inside, you sigh.

time seems different in the room. a film of green-yellow aging covers everything in sight, and you tense your jaw noticing holes in your vision. tiny ones, barely there. they flicker like tunnels. you think of where they could lead, what spiraling stairways you could climb - you picture spires. they feel endless. as you stare out at the vases and empty photo frames, words form in your mind. the tunnel is a tower.

you're in the snow again, footsteps behind you for miles. icicles are growing from the ground. hail is beginning to fall, but when you look into the white expanse, ice seems to only be falling where you're standing. an icicle in front of you splinters into flaked mirrors, reflecting a grey eye in its shards.

rubbing your eyes as if fresh out of sleep, you turn an eye upwards. you freeze at the terrible vision above you. then you run, kicking up clouds with the momentum. the world is moving with you, moving too, moving faster than you - the eyes that follow, they hang still in the sky, glazed and heavy.

sunlight didn't used to feel like this. how much further can you go? the grasses around your feet seem comfortable in death. the swelling of the ground makes you grimace. your dark circles ache; you know the earth is coated in rust.

a slow-running river should be peaceful - water shouldn't sound so unsoft. but the trickle cascades and the sweet birds scream and you lay by the water. you reach out to dip a finger in the current. you feel thick ice instead.

you don't know how it happened. one moment you're on the riverbank, the next you claw at the ice from below, palms pressed flat. pushing. the water is a slurry. your eyes are bloodshot. blurred visions of floating things are all you see across the sheet of ice holding you under. surrounded by water on all sides, your skin feels burned.

slowly. you go down slowly, slower than you should with arms of lead. your body crumples, frays at the edges - in the currents, movements are infinite. your descent stutters, no end. no beginning. every time you're certain the floor will catch you, the ice is back on your palms. how much further can you go? the air has run out. you're still here.

your body is an artifact.

Leak 04-13 (Bait Ones) Jai Paul, 2019) review by Daniel Flores

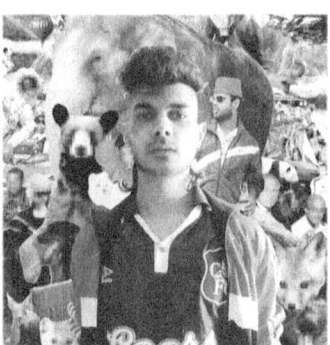

[best enjoyed while playing "Genevieve (unfinished)" in the background]

I find myself in awe while paying attention to all the sonic details in this album, and how they work together in each song to build its specific mood in unexpected or backward ways that still feel digestible, danceable, fun, and very familiar. "All Night (unfinished)" is so watery and feels healing in a way, "Desert River (unfinished)" is like a futuristic jungle, "Jasmine (unfinished)" is trippy and larger than life; like the album cover, the project feels like a vivid digital collage.

I also think that for such an experimental project with plenty of sampling and unlikely combinations of textures, it boasts some of the best music ever made to be played while in a car at night: addictive rhythms, catchy vocals, and boomy bass are some of the elements that drive a big chunk of this project, and these are used in ways I had never heard before, while at the same time achieving their purpose better than most popular club music of the time, just listen to Jai's cover of Jennifer Paige's record "Crush" from 1998, the bass is something else. This album's mix of Bollywood samples, groovy aquatic electric guitar riffs, hypnotic synth chords and melodies, and layers of (sometimes unpolished) vocals create a soundscape that I often crave to revisit because of how unique it is.

This album is very important for me because it's thought-provoking and inspiring, not only in its contents but also its history, thinking about Jai's endless hours choosing samples, sound-designing synths, getting the best vocal takes possible, mixing the instruments, trying out different effects, etc. just for all of that focus and care to be casually interrupted by his laptop getting robbed and the incomplete album getting leaked online is a sort of cautionary tale for me, perfectionism is often my enemy when it comes to art, I get obsessed with the details. As I work on finishing my band's EP, I realize that at any point something unfortunate could happen to me as it did to Jai Paul, as artists, we capture the essence of the present and we must catch the present before it is no more. Art is not necessarily urgent, but it does change with time. We must act like a baseball batter and hit the ball at the perfect time where our effort/satisfaction is balanced the most.

Thinking about this album I also realize how, whether we like it or not, our art exists on its own, it says things that we didn't command it to, and it gets involved in dialogues we don't understand. Worrying about being understood obsessively is futile. Maybe by leaving blanks to be filled (maybe intentionally, not on accident like Jai), we can experience our creativity in more fulfilling ways. The lyrics throughout "Bait Ones" can be retrospectively analyzed knowing the record's history. Doing so makes the project far grander and more meaningful, especially on "BTSTU", the last track:

[Verse 2]
The ship was the love of my life
We went down together that night
I surfaced in every shadow
For years I just kotched on the down low
[Chorus]
I know I've been gone a long time
I'm back and I want what is mine
I know I've been gone a long time
I'm back and I want what is mine

Lyrics that normally would just be about a complicated romantic relationship can be taken into the context of Jai Paul "going down together that night" along with his leaked magnum opus, going into the dark and staying low after the leak until he eventually did an official digital and physical release 6 years later in 2019, "taking back what's his". such readings on the lyrical content are also strong in "Zion Wolf Theme (unfinished)", "Genevieve (unfinished)", and "100,000 (unfinished)". Lyrics that work at multiple levels and messy production as a positive trait are both elements that I try to apply in my work, and I'm grateful for discovering this project because it helped me learn more about them.

I find it sad how a stolen laptop incident robbed us of more of Jai's music, robbed Jai of his deserved success and notoriety, robbed the culture of art that could've pushed our collective boundaries as listeners and artists ever so slightly beyond where they currently sit, but in a way I enjoy appreciating a project this beautiful in the context of such a complicated history that speaks to me personally as a creator, for me that makes it much more.

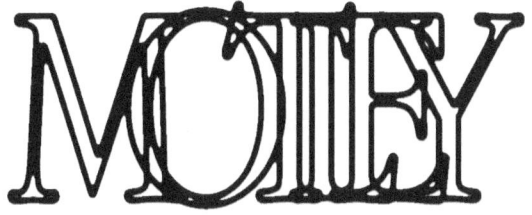

MOTLEY MAG
WILL HAVE A
FIFTH
VOLUME

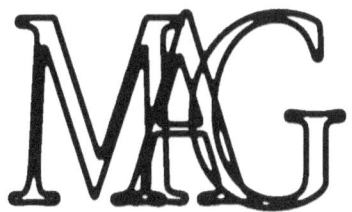

www.ingramcontent.com/pod-product-compliance
Lightning Source LLC
Chambersburg PA
CBHW030014190526
45157CB00016B/2771